"Philip Harris has provided us  ok-
ing view into the words spoke ecret"
and despite having shared his d but
didn't listen. This book will ma and
realize just how powerful the words of Jesus really were. No
matter what your religious beliefs are this book will educate you
to not just hear, but to listen and to apply what it is that you learn,
allowing you the capability of having a bountiful and prosperous
today and every day thereafter."
Katrina Stiles, Alternative-Read.com (UK)

"In his thought provoking new book, *Jesus Taught It, Too: The
Early Roots of The Law of Attraction*, Phil Harris takes his reader
back 2000 years to explore the early roots of The Law of Attraction
using the words of Jesus Christ himself. Phil builds a strong case
while providing insightful interpretations of Jesus' message which
demonstrate the Law of Attraction is not new and certainly no
"Secret"."
Vicki Link, www.youcreatereality.com

"Phil Harris takes the essence of archaic religious wisdom, and
interprets a realistic translation and transition to current spiritual
principles. He provides the insight and rationality to empower
ourselves in today's world.
Brilliant, Inspiring and Insightful!"
**Steven Mayber, Transformational Healer,
www.globalhealingsolutions.com**

"Your book is a profound; highly compelling piece of work…
compelling one to wake up from the dogma machinery… it
should raise many eyebrows! And create some religious
constipation!"
Ed Rychkun

The Law of Attraction is no newly revealed secret, it was taught by a very humble man of God more than 2000 years ago. "Jesus Taught It, Too: The Early Roots of the Law of Attraction," by Philip Harris presents a compelling argument that the Law of Attraction is not a modern paradigm shift. Harris puts forth that the teachings of Jesus and his followers is a mindset that requires knowing one's inner meaning that comes from the heart. Jesus espoused the firm belief that faith is based on knowing…not hoping.

Harris' in-depth research of Biblical scripture and history offers well-founded premises to support his discussion of Jesus' simple message. According to Harris, Jesus taught that the reality of the world is that we live in a unified universe, free of judgment, seeking our spirituality. Organized religion is a man-made institution that teaches the faithful about the dogma of good, evil, sin and a punitive God. The New Age movement is not truly new, according to Harris, since the early 1800's the movement of positive thinking and positive affirmations has included the likes of Alcott, Emerson and Thoreau. Man has sought to analyze spiritual thought and seek their inner Christ through visualization since the Apostles sat at the foot of their Master.

"Jesus Taught It, Too…" explores the concept that a true meditative state is found only when you are free of emotional, spiritual, and physical baggage. Through the recognition that God is not exclusionary you can reap physical, spiritual, mental, and emotional wealth. Doubt will ensure failure.

"Jesus Taught It, Too…" presents complex theocratic beliefs in simple, straight-forward language. The Law of Attraction addresses the powerful influence of positive thinking in the acquisition of physical and material needs. Jesus taught that by applying these same principals to one's spiritual life, one's physical and material needs will be met as a natural result of their application. Harris challenges the reader to "believe in the best with an inner conviction…and it will manifest in your life."

This book's intriguing but down-to-earth message will appeal to any reader seeking to broaden their spiritual horizon.

This is a must read for those that are the true believers of Jesus Christ. Mr. Harris went beyond what the church would want you to know of Jesus as a philosophical human being, with knowledge not only in spirituality, but also of the true meaning behind the words. If you have been following the church and what they want you to believe blindly, then it is time to stop being just another one of the many sheep and become an individual power that can and will draw others into the truth of Jesus. This book is your start to that truth which will only grow with your new outlook upon the words of Jesus.
Troy Hite

For those who reject the secret of the universe in favor of religious speculation, here's a sermon of universal truth from the master prophet Himself. There will be no denying this evidence. From the agnostic to the evangelical, if this doesn't convince you, nothing will. Harris' work is easy to read and digest. He offers sometimes complex ideas in accessible ways so that any reader of any age can grasp the meaning of his words. This is a remarkable read, a must-read.
 Brian Doe, Co-Author, WAKING GOD, Author, Barley and Gold

The Law of Attraction is not a newly revealed secret, it was taught by a very humble man of God more than 2000 years ago. "Jesus Taught It, Too: The Early Roots of the Law of Attraction," by Philip Harris presents a compelling argument that the Law of Attraction is not a modern paradigm shift. Harris portrays the teachings of Jesus and his followers as a mindset that requires knowing one's inner meaning that comes from the heart. Jesus, referenced in multiple scriptural references, espoused the firm belief that faith is based on knowing...not hoping.

Harris' in-depth research of Biblical scripture and history offers unique perspectives and well-founded premises to support his discussion of Jesus' simple message. According to Harris, Jesus taught that we live in a unified universe, free of judgment, in which we are seeking our individual spirituality. Organized religion is a man-made institution that teaches the faithful about the dogma of good, evil, sin and a punitive God. The New Age movement is not truly new, according to Harris. Since the early 1800's the movement has taught the power of positive thinking and positive affirmations and has included such followers as Alcott, Emerson and Thoreau. Man has sought to analyze spiritual thought and seek their inner Christ through visualization since the Apostles first sat at the foot of their Master.

"Jesus Taught It, Too..." explores the concept that a true meditative state is found only when you are free of emotional, spiritual, and physical baggage. Through the recognition that God is not exclusionary you can reap physical, spiritual, mental, and emotional wealth. Doubt will ensure failure.

"Jesus Taught It, Too..." presents complex theocratic beliefs in simple, straight-forward language. The Law of Attraction addresses the powerful influence of positive thinking in the acquisition of physical and material needs. Jesus taught that by applying these same principals to one's spiritual life, one's physical and material needs will be met as a natural result of their application. Harris challenges the reader to "believe in the best with an inner conviction...and it will manifest in your life." This book's intriguing but down-to-earth message will appeal to any reader seeking to broaden their spiritual horizon.

Shannon Evans "My Writing Mentor" (Seattle, WA)

"Jesus Taught It, Too is truly a beautiful book - and I rarely use the word beautiful when it comes to books! I just couldn't put it down - the combination of the message of Jesus along with Philip Harris' way of putting it in written prose is really like music to the soul. You'll just want to read it again and again."
Ahmed Jamal, who lives in Jordan.

Excellent Book!!! It was a true awakening for me. Excellent way of explaining the law of attraction! I really enjoyed reading this book.
Marina Chakhalyan

Philip Harris has provided us with an inspiring, thought provoking view into the words spoken by Jesus, who knew The Secret and despite having shared his knowledge freely, many heard but didn't listen. This book will make you stand up on your toes and realize just how powerful the words of Jesus really were. No matter what your religious beliefs are this book will educate you to not just hear, but to listen and to apply what it is that you learn, allowing you the capability of having a bountiful and prosperous today and every day thereafter.
Katrina Stiles "WritingWithStiles (New Port Richey, FL)

In a day and age where "Jesus" and "God" have practically become four letter words, author Harris dares to dig into the Bible and present Jesus to modern man in a new, non-traditional (in organized Christian church terms) fashion. Harris is a very innovative spiritualist writer, and he has done another fine job in producing this work. Drawing strictly on the quotes of Jesus from the traditionally accepted books in the New Testament of the Bible, he reveals Jesus to the reader as having been not just the appointed savior of man, but also a teacher of each and every human being's own innate birthright of godhood.

Just what *was* Jesus trying to tell us?

The quoted words of Jesus in the Bible are by no means enigmatic; they are rather simple and straight forward. However, they can be interpreted in many different ways, on different levels. Right off the top, they can instruct us on how to live an ethical, moral, upright life. Digging further into them, they can lead us to an understanding of how to get beyond our selfishness and love everyone, even our enemies, as our own self. In "Jesus Taught It, Too! (The Early Roots of the Law of Attraction)," author Phil Harris has given us a stellar and insightful interpretation of Jesus as the Master Teacher who pointed out the Way to those who "have ears to hear," on an even deeper level; that being a roadmap to not just *following* Christ and becoming "Christ-like," but rather the self-discovery of all that we are, and that being nothing other than God Itself. There is just as much inner space as outer-space, and our sense of "I Am," our conscious free will, is a swinging door opening up heaven or hell as we create either one with our thoughts and desires.

Very well written, well thought through, and with lots of added spiritual treats at the end of Harris' expose, this book is a timely read, riding the crest of the current global interest in the **Law of Attraction**. Twenty or thirty years ago, this work would most likely have been dubbed as "esoteric" by the majority, but I believe that is not apropos in today's climate of growing non-exclusive spiritual interest across the planet. This book is a valuable addition to anyone's library who considers him or her self as a real investigator of spiritual truth. Probably a bit too over the top for anyone with literal mindedness or traditional fundamentalist Christian beliefs, but for those with an open mind, *I highly recommend it!*
Marvin D. Wilson, author, I ROMANCED THE STONE, OWEN FIDDLER

JESUS TAUGHT IT, TOO!

THE EARLY ROOTS OF THE LAW OF ATTRACTION

PHILIP F. HARRIS

JESUS TAUGHT IT, TOO!

THE EARLY ROOTS OF THE LAW OF ATTRACTION

ISBN: 0-9822056-0-0

ISBN 13: 978-0-9822056-0-0

Library of Congress Number: 2008910153

Previously published in 2007 by Avatar Publications
ISBN: 978-0-9780969-6-0

Cover Design by All Things That Matter Press

Published in 2008 by All Things That Matter Press
Printed in the United States of America

DEDICATION

To those who need the words of the past
as a guide to their future;
To my friends Kathy, Andrea, Cindy, and
A BELIEVER IN FAERIES
And,
As always and for always,
To Deb

Table of Contents

INTRODUCTION

The world is being increasingly exposed to challenges to traditional religious thought. The film and book, "The Secret," the release of "The Gospel of Judas," the film, "The Lost Tomb of Jesus," the book "The End of Faith" by Sam Harris, and the novel, "Waking God" by authors Doe and Harris are but a small example of the onslaught directed at religious dogma. With publicity for these new ideas being heralded by Larry King, Oprah and DeGeneres as well as the exponential increase in the number of web sites, blogs and forums regarding the Law of Attraction and manifesting your own reality, religious institutions are facing their greatest trials since the Reformation.

Added to this siege are the frequent and highly publicized church scandals. Issues of gay ministers, the right of clergy to marriage, potential schisms and the role of women in the various churches have been frequent page one headlines. Some would label these The End Times or End of Days. Others would argue that this is not an end, but a beginning of a New Age of Spirituality. The latter would say that we are in a "time of questioning" that will lead humanity to a new level of understanding between humanity and the Cosmos. Quantum science is peering into the very fabric of reality and discovering that appearances have long been deceiving. Rather than disproving the claim of Intelligent Design, science may yet prove that behind all that we term reality is a guiding consciousness.

People are beginning to question the interpretation of holy texts, and new archeological discoveries are raising doubts over what was held my many as historical fact. Was Jesus married? Did he leave behind physical remains? Did early religious leaders and messengers actually tell of a stream of thought that is far different from what has been preached in the pulpit? Are religious teachings really about worship, the struggle of good versus evil and the concept of sin and punishment or do they describe a unified Universe where there is duality without judgment and a blueprint for the spiritual evolution of humanity?

While dogma and institution have certainly come under fire, the actual teachings of early religious leaders have not. While those who may have distorted and skewed teachings have been backed against the wall, the messages of the early Masters are receiving revived interest and new interpretations. What are emerging are new sets of Spiritual Laws that contradict common theological "wisdom." These Laws are common threads found in all religious texts but which have, for millennia, been downplayed or kept secret.

The "new spirituality" is not at all new. The late 1800's and early 1900's saw new views of the Universe in existentialism, transcendentalism and theosophy. The writings of H. Spencer Lewis, often overlooked, began to make known some of the secrets held within the Rose Cross. Since then, there have been books on everything from creating wealth to thinking yourself well. In the sixties there was the emergent guru and music of that time was filled with spiritual messages. The 80's witnessed the New Age movement and many flocked to their daily dose of affirmations, positive thinking and messages from beyond that flowed into willing "channelers."

Today we have moved beyond "positive thinking" as new revelations and secrets are being revealed to millions over the Internet and through mass media outlets. At the same time, we are witnessing the growth of religious fundamentalism as the old institutions and ways of thinking try to maintain their historical sway on the minds and hearts of the former faithful. As in the days of the Reformation, the lines of spiritual thought have been drawn in the sand, sometimes with blood.

"JESUS TAUGHT IT, TOO" is not an attempt to revive or support traditional Christian thought. On the contrary, it presents a unique interpretation of the sayings of the Master that stand in juxtaposition to conventional religious thought. This work shows that most of the literature regarding such topics as the Law of Attraction, The Manifestation Process, creating one's reality, thinking and growing rich and visualizing your way to goal fulfillment date back over two thousand years. The founding principles of all of these lines of spiritual thought can be found in the Christian Bible in the actual words of the one named Jesus. This is not to infer that Jesus was the only ancient messenger to lay the foundation for current spiritual thought, but it clearly shows is that He did lay such a foundation.

It is also clear that the way pointed out by Jesus is not what is commonly taught to the masses. Just praying to Jesus and proclaiming him your personal savior will not invoke the Law of Attraction or the Manifestation Process. This fact is borne out by history. Getting to the "Father," the kingdom within, through the acceptance of the inner Christ, and not the man, Jesus, is the path that one must follow. This path is open to all that will accept that a higher state of being exists at the core of our essence. It can be called the

Christ, higher self, or any term one chooses. The key is to recognize that within each of us is a power that is the same that created the Universe. It is this power that we utilize to manifest all that we desire.

CHAPTER ONE

It has been said that "the meek shall inherit the earth." It has not been said that the poor, the sick, the depressed, the hungry, the downtrodden or even the followers of a particular religion will inherit the earth. "Meek" simply means "showing mildness" or displaying a "quietness of nature." Yet for thousands of years that one phrase has been used to justify the exploitation of millions. Humanity has been told to suffer its lot in life because if you do, great rewards will be bestowed upon you after death.

Religious dogma has done little to advance the cause of humanity. While followers of various faiths have often worked to alleviate the suffering of many, the actual institutions have been the cause of war and divisiveness throughout the ages. The irony is that the teachings of the great Masters, which unfortunately led to institutionalized religions, actually left wonderful roadmaps aimed at improving both the material and the spiritual status of humanity. These maps have often been hidden, passed over, or misinterpreted in the interests of maintaining the power and privilege of a few.
It has also been said that "all that is hidden will be revealed."

Beginning in the 19th Century, many came forward offering new interpretations of ancient secrets, the universe and ways for humanity to gain material and spiritual advancement. Prior to this time, the wisdom that would free humanity from its dogmatic yoke lay hidden in secret texts, kept alive by so called "secret societies," or even hidden in plain sight in paintings, decks of cards, architecture and in the form of plays, poetry and works of literature. All that was needed to unlock the guides to human advancement were mysterious keys and codes or a willingness to explore the inner meanings of carefully chosen phrases and passages. The need for secrecy was mandated, since those who held the reins of power were willing to do anything to prevent higher knowledge from reaching the minds of the masses. Inquisitions, genocides, mass torture, and all sorts of unspeakable methods were used to prevent the dissemination of the truth and to maintain the secrecy of this higher wisdom.

Despite all of the grand efforts to censor the truth, much has remained readily available to those who seek a greater understanding of humanity's relationship to the COSMOS. After all, if the teachings of the great masters and avatars were totally suppressed, there would be no basis for the dogma that has for so long held sway over the thoughts of man. Still, even though "truths" have been at our disposal at all times, it is incredible that those in power have still been able to assert such control. Throughout the millennia, those who sat at the apex of religious institutions have been able to convince the masses that it is only they who have the key to the meaning of scripture and verse.

Times have changed. Arising from the early teachings of Theosophy, the early spiritualists and the "New Age" phenomena, barriers to free religious thinking are crumbling like the once invincible Berlin Wall. In our era of instant communication, it has become almost impossible to censor or control the spread of new ideas and enlightened thinking. A generally literate world population, mass media outlets, TV, the Internet, YouTube and the dwindling capacity of religious leaders to impose penalties upon dissenting thought has resulted in a spiritual revolution that appears unstoppable. These institutions are under daily siege and their foundation is showing major cracks. People are re-reading religious texts and finding new and personal meanings in the words of the masters. Unencumbered by the chains of the self-proclaimed moral authorities, a new-found inner freedom and understanding of spiritual thought is sweeping across the world.

CHAPTER TWO

We are all familiar with the name Jeshua Ben Joseph, commonly referred to as Jesus. His thoughts and ideas altered the course of human history and formed the basis of the institution that became known as Christianity. This book is not about his history. It does not address the issue of his existence, nor does it examine alternative texts and scripture that were deleted or suppressed by religious authorities. Since it is the accepted Bible that has formed the basis of religious dogma, it is best to reference that which has been "accepted" as containing the words of Jesus rather than to debate other possible and probable sources of his teaching. Thus the teachings discussed in this book come from the King James Version of the Bible. Like the "purloined letter," the wisdom of the Master Jesus has been before us all, awaiting a new interpretation and a new vision in thought.

Jesus was by no means the first to introduce the concept of the Law of Attraction. If one were to examine the works of the ancient mystics, it would be clear that the Law had its earliest roots in ancient Egypt and Babylon. However, few are familiar with the likes of the Pharaoh Akhenaton and fewer still with mystical thoughts of the rest of the ancient world. The Jewish Kabala is another source of information on the Law of Attraction, and it is said that many "secret societies" like the Rose Cross have long kept the old mysteries and laws alive throughout the centuries. One could just as easily focus upon the teachings of Buddha or Lao Tzu and the Law would be revealed in that spiritual context. Further examination of the Bhagavad-Gita and the Mahabharata also reveal the same

Laws and thus support the claim that it is universal in nature and in origin.

The sayings of Jesus presented in this work are taken in the order in which they appear in the Bible. If they are essentially the same from one gospel to the next, the interpretation is not repeated unless some important nuance is detected. Sayings presented are those that this author feels represent the early public roots of what has become called "The Law of Attraction." Upon close examination, an additional law, "The Law of Responsibility" also emerges as an integral part of the Master's philosophy. These are my interpretations and I do not presume to be a higher authority regarding the meanings of the sayings. By the same token, I am no lesser an authority. We all have the ability to seek and find the inner meaning of scripture, regardless of religious persuasion. I make little effort to describe the context of the quotes as in many cases; the context is inconsequential to the interpretation of the meaning. What is important is the stream of thought that is revealed in the teachings of Jesus with respect to the subject at hand. It is important to view the entire thread pertaining to the spiritual laws of Jesus if one is to reach any kind of reasonable conclusion regarding his thoughts on the subject.

There are three levels of interpretation that are employed when attempting to analyze spiritual thought. The first level is an objective analysis. The results of this mode of thinking are literal conclusions regarding concepts. Fundamentalists are prone to this way of thinking. The second level is the subjective. This tends to delve a little deeper and answers the question, "What does this passage mean to me?" This line of analysis is generally based upon your own life experience regarding the concept at hand in which biases and your personal belief systems form the basis of your conclusions. The next level is the inner or spiritual meaning. It is here that few travel, as most have been told the "meaning" by a pastor or priest. This path requires the removal of personal bias and conditioning and demands that the mind open to the influx of deeper spiritual insight. It is the inner voice that speaks at this level and the result is often personal revelation. The historical accumulations of such revelations that have been consistent throughout the ages form the body of works that we know of as "The Secret Teachings."

CHAPTER THREE

The Law of Attraction is not just about the acquisition of things. Much of the recent criticism surrounding such phenomena as the film and the book "The Secret" is that the concept is egocentric and too materialistic. Yes, the Law of Attraction does deal with humanity's material needs and desires but it also focuses upon humanity's spiritual needs. Detractors, utilizing the scare tactics of old, attempt to cast this idea as anti-spiritual, something other than godly, and bordering on satanic. At first glance, the first quote discussed would appear to support the contention of the critics.

"Take these things hence; make not my Father's house a house of merchandise."

Many are probably familiar with the story of when Jesus threw the money changers out of the Temple. Some would say that based upon the above, material things have no place in spiritual teachings. Out of context with the entire stream of thought, it could be argued that detractors are correct. Even though the plate is passed every Sunday, and the Catholic Church is one of the richest and most powerful organizations in the world, they would say that things of this world should be shunned. However, there is another way to look at this quote and that is that Jesus was talking about our own consciousness and that, in that context, Jesus was saying that when you are focused upon higher spiritual thoughts, it is appropriate to not be concerned with the troubles, the cares and the physical burdens of your life. To think clearly one must remove the "merchandise" or excess baggage from the mind in order to gain a clear focus. This is a part of any true meditative state and enables one to focus upon the work at hand.

"Say not ye, there are yet four months, and then cometh harvest? Behold, I say unto you, Lift up your eyes, and look on the fields; for they are white already to harvest. And he that reapeth receiveth wages, and gathereth fruit unto life eternal: that both he that soweth and he that reapeth may rejoice together."

This is perhaps the first saying that directly begins the discussion of the unlimited abundance that is readily available to all. Fundamentalists will be quick to claim that this is a reference to the "word of God" and has nothing to do with material needs and wants. That is one interpretation and it is also partially correct, but one must bear in mind that Jesus also ate, drank, and sustained his material body with material sustenance.

The powerful people of this world would have us believe that resources are limited and that we must be thankful for anything that we have. Religious authorities, who are often awash in worldly riches, also promote the scarcity of resources fear, but promise that greater riches will be awarded to those who are faithful to their doctrine. After all, if everyone sought the riches of others, conflict would arise. In fact, this has historically been the case. The Age of Exploration was all about finding gold and wealth. The Colonial Age was about controlling the resources of other "less advanced" nations. Many will recall the Nazi demand for living space, and the Industrial Revolution generated war and conflict as the corporate machines demanded the natural resources of others. We are all too familiar with notion of the "have and the have nots."

Jesus is saying that there is no scarcity. All that we could possibly desire is already available and waiting to be claimed. The money is in the bank in our name and all that is needed is the withdrawal slip. Who is "he that soweth?" The sower is the mind. The disciples did not see the fields ripe with harvest with their physical eyes. Jesus was telling them to lift their eyes, open their minds and with their inner vision truly see and visualize the harvest. Abundance is always available. Of course, because we live on the physical plane, we are also the reaper of the harvest. We must take physical action to reap the harvest we have sown with our opened eyes and our mind.

This is the art of visualization. See what is desired, not in the future, but in the now. See what is desired as manifest in the now and develop a mindset that is ready to harvest the mental crop. Jesus did not say, "See the harvest being planted." He did not say, "Watch the crop grow." He said, "The fields are ready to harvest."

When the mind and the body work together, when mind and matter work as one, we will have all that we need as long as we live. There are no limits, there is no scarcity and there is no need to take from others, since all that we desire is available in the mental fields that are "white with harvest."

What you see in your mind, you attract on the physical plane.

CHAPTER FOUR

A "judgment" is a final decision. There is much confusion regarding the following quote, as many have interpreted the lines in terms of the passing of a verdict or a condemnation. On the contrary, this saying is at the heart of the Law of Attraction.

"JUDGE not, that ye be not judged. For with what judgment ye judge, ye shall be judged: and with what measure ye mete, it shall be measured to you again."

Let's rephrase the saying with the concept of a final decision in mind. _Do not make a final decision so that a final decision is not made about your life._ Whatever you make a final decision about is the course your life will take. Whatever you decide about the world, that is the way your world will be.

The Law of Attraction says that what you hold in thought and imbue with emotion and intent is what will manifest in your life. If you have made a "final decision" that the world is a place of pain, suffering and despair, then that is how the world will be measured back to you. If you hold in your mind disease, that will be measured back to you. If you hold in your mind poverty, that is what the world will return. If you hold hatred, bigotry, violence and failure, these things will be in your life. If you hold fear, then your life will manifest all the things that you fear.

How often are we admonished that appearances are deceiving? How often do we perceive an event in a negative way only to discover that it was a blessing in disguise? Have you ever felt dislike towards a person only to later become best friends? Have you ever been disappointed about a job loss only to end up with an even better job?

When we close our minds to new information and new ideas, we close off the manifesting power of the Universe. When we say "This is the way life is," the Universe continues to reinforce our final decision about life and provides all the things and events that go along with that decision.

Life isn't fair? Times are tough? I do not know what to do? The world is out to get me? I'll never get out of this rut? I am not smart enough? I do not have enough money? I am not attractive enough? If any of these are your outlook on life, the Universe will return to you a life that contains most, if not all, of these decisions.

We never have complete information. Even in science, what is true today is superceded tomorrow. What would have happened if the early sciences were held to be true and, as a result, further research was halted? Nothing that we know today would exist. There would be no heart transplants, no vaccines, no CT scans, no X-rays, and no progress in all of the areas of technology that we take for granted. Science remains open and positive about its own progress and yet, when it comes to our personal lives, we form opinions and judgments and final decisions and remain passive in the face of "fate" to the point that only an act of God will change our minds. It is only when we open to the influx of new ideas and concepts that the Universe offers a variety of ways to provide for our needs and desires.

Jesus healed others because he refused to accept the illusion. He made no decision based upon appearances and saw what we would call the sick as whole and well. He held in his mind the truth that we are all whole, and his thoughts became manifest.

If he had judged the sick to be sick, he would not have been able to manifest the truth. This is the same with each of us. If we see through the illusion of pain and suffering, we are in a position to assist ourselves and to better serve those in need. If we see the world as a place filled with infinite possibilities and opportunities, then we open ourselves to those possibilities. If we judge something as evil or bad, we actually create a reality that contains evil and bad. If we see someone suffering and adopt an "oh, poor you" attitude, then we have judged that person as beyond repair.

Does this mean that you lose all compassion? On the contrary, it means that by seeing the poor as wealthy, the sick as whole, the depressed as happy and the wicked as good, we create a new vibration that can and will bring those qualities into existence. You have to ask yourself, which is more compassionate, feeling pity for the suffering or actually creating a reality where suffering does not exist?

Incidentally, this is why we are admonished to be "born again." Enter each day with new eyes and no preconceived notions. Enter the day with an expectation that all will be right, and the Universe will fulfill that expectation. This is not easy. We are the products of a conditioning that fills our subconscious mind with the "merchandise" of the world. We carry over into each morning all of our hopes, dreams and fears. But, day-by-day, we can make progress, and with each step the world becomes a brighter place. Look adversity in the face and say "No, you no longer control the way I perceive life. I will not decide if what is happening is positive or negative. I will let the Universe unfold new ideas and new opportunities and will see each moment as an opportunity to learn and to grow. I lack complete information and what may appear to be negative may be the best thing that could happen to me."

Gradually, day by day, old thought habits will diminish and a new paradigm, a new outlook on life, will bring more positive events into your life.

"The time is fulfilled, and the kingdom of God is at hand: repent ye, and believe the gospel. Repent: for the kingdom of God is at hand."

Repent means to change your ways or change your mind. The *Kingdom of God is here, believe in this truth, change your way of thinking, for the Kingdom of God is here.*

This is a different way of looking at these words of Jesus than priests would present. Here we are being asked to change the way we think about things, change our outlook on the world. We are not being asked to ask for forgiveness. We are to understand the truth that heaven is on earth now, not some day in the future.
Religious leaders have convinced the masses that heaven is a future state of existence, in some distant location in a galaxy far, far away. They tell us that this is hell on earth and if we are good and ask no questions, we may receive our just reward.

But the good shepherd gave a different message. Heaven is available to all in the NOW, this very moment, if we but repent, change our minds, and accept the truth. The fields are already white with harvest and it is a change in our mindset that will lift our eyes to see this truth.

CHAPTER FIVE

It is not that people should show off their successes, but neither should they hide them. Teaching by example has long been touted as a way to convince others of the correctness of the way you live and think.

"Ye are the light of the world. A city that is set on a hill cannot be hid. Neither do men light a candle, and put it under a bushel, but on a candlestick; and it giveth light unto all that are in the house. Let your light so shine before men, that they may see your good works. And glorify your Father which is in heaven."

It should be obvious from the above quote that Jesus did not think that humanity was the scum of the earth. He did not believe we were poor wretched creatures, full of sin, worthy of punishment, and fit for nothing but hiding under a stone. There is no question that this is a reference to our spiritual light, but it also deals with every aspect of our life, including our material nature.

The Law of Attraction proclaims that all people are imbued with the creative power of the Universe. Just as our children share many of our traits, the children of the Universe have the same light as that which created them. In a way, it is "in the genes." By proclaiming that all are the "light of the world," Jesus was saying that it is wrong to hide or suppress our true nature. By letting our light shine, we are claiming our relationship to our divinity. By expressing what is inherently ours, we are actually paying homage to that force that permeates the entire universe. All parents want the best for their children right? All parents, no matter how "divine," want their children to succeed, to find happiness, to be "healthy, wealthy and wise." What kind of parent wishes eternal suffering on his children?

Why would anyone think or even promote the notion that we, the "children of God" are not meant to have health, prosperity, and abundant love? Those that do foster these beliefs are usually ones who have achieved a degree of success but fear that others will take that from them. It is this belief in scarcity that fosters the limited and constricting ideas of the world. It is as if they are saying that there can be only so many healthy, wealthy and happy people in the world and if you are not one of them, be content with what you have and you will receive your reward in heaven. Does this not sound like a conflict of interest? It is said in The Secret that not everyone wants the same job, the same life partner or wants to live exactly as someone else. There is enough to go around. If, as science says, all things are made of energy, there is certainly an abundance of energy in the Universe to go around. Let's face it, they can always print more money. Therefore, let the light that you are find expression and finally end the illusion of darkness.

"Be ye therefore perfect, even as your Father which is in heaven is perfect."

If humanity is fatally flawed, why would Jesus say that you can achieve the perfection of the divine intelligence that created the Universe? By saying that deity is the Father of all, it follows that we are all equally the sons and daughters of God. There are no exclusionary notions in this quote. No one is left out of the equation. Jesus does not say try to be perfect, he says be perfect.

Somewhere along the way someone decided that it would be best for people to think that they were essentially evil and that only by maintaining adherence to certain creeds and dogma would they find salvation. By doing this, people have used this perceived lack of perfection as an excuse to explain all the evils of the world. It has been used to justify and rationalize why some are in misery while others flourish.

The Law of Attraction says that people are perfect in potential and all that stands between the truth and the reality is a state of mind. Is this not what Jesus is saying? There is no indication in his admonition that anything should stand in the way of human perfection. He did not say, "Try to be like me because I am the only son of God and I am perfect and even though you are all sinners, you just might improve your life." The use of the word "BE" is a command, not a request. Jesus chose his words carefully and was not prone to exaggeration. I also believe that Jesus did not contradict himself and that he meant exactly what he said. BE the conscious creative force in your world and create your new reality based in Light and perfection.

CHAPTER SIX

"Therefore I say unto you, Take no thought for your life, what ye shall eat, or what ye shall drink; nor yet for your body, what ye shall put on. Is not the life more than meat, and the body than raiment? Behold the fowls of the air: for they sow not, neither do they reap, nor gather into barns; yet your heavenly Father feedeth them. Are ye not much better than they?"

The above and the passages that follow are truly the heart and soul of the Law of Attraction. In my mind there is no room for misinterpretation.

Take no thought for your life.

Be not concerned for food or drink.

Care not about clothing.

Do not be concerned how these things will come.

The Universe provides for all of your needs. As far as Jesus is concerned, all that you need to sustain life is available and freely provided. This raises the obvious question about shortages and the fact that people live in poverty, starve to death and are homeless. Some people would have us believe that this happens because not all people are Christian and must suffer the consequence. Of course, I am not sure that sparrows attend church or that they have proclaimed their faith in God, yet they seem to deserve life.

Humanity is convinced that there are lack and limits in this world. They believe that there is not enough wealth, food or shelter to meet basic needs. This myth has been perpetuated for thousands of years by both secular and sectarian authorities to the point where most of the people in the world are convinced that this is true. As a result, since reality follows thought, we have the illusionary manifestation of lack and insufficiency. We all know that there is food enough for all. We all know that everyone could be sheltered and clothed. We all know that there is enough abundance on this planet to end suffering, misery and pain. We all know that the end to these perceived problems is only a thought a way.

Unless Jesus lied, the fields are already white with harvest. Do humans have to labor to satisfy their basic needs? At the present time in our evolution, I would have to say yes. Is this a requirement of the Universe? I do not believe that it is. If we let our light shine and *Become* the perfection of our true being, the provision of needs and the fulfillment of desires can be achieved with mental effort and minimal "sweat of the brow."

Was not water turned to wine? Were not the masses fed with but a few loaves of bread and a few fish? We all have the power to do this, according to Jesus and all of the other great avatars. Once the myth of limitation is wiped from our subconscious memories, all this becomes possible.

"Which of you by taking thought can add one cubit unto his stature? And why take ye thought for raiment? Consider the lilies of the field, how they grow; they toil not, neither do they spin: and yet I say unto you, That even Solomon in all his glory was not arrayed like one of these. Wherefore, if God so clothe the grass of the field, which today is, and tomorrow is cast into the oven, shall he not much more clothe you, O ye of little faith?"

You cannot become what you are not. You cannot un-think yourself. We ignore the fact that the Universe has chosen to teach by its own example. Nature is in a state of balance. What goes into the system is equal to what comes out of the system. Energy changes form and appearance, and yet the system is self perpetuating. Each year brings new life that is built upon the old life that seems to pass away. But the perception of death is again, illusion. All things return to the energy that they are and take form once again to express what appears to be new life.

It is the same with us. There is no need to worry about the source of our sustenance. It is by worrying that we create the illusion of lack while all the while there is ample energy to provide for our needs. Our thoughts may create the appearance that we have created shortages and that scarcity exists, but by taking thought in this manner we cannot alter the stature of the Universe.

Abundance exists regardless of appearances. Perfection exists regardless of our notions to the contrary. What is given to the lily is given freely. What is given to us is also given freely. Even when we appear to disrupt the balance, all we have done is to alter the form in which energy is stored. Our actions do not change the truth of nature.

Science teaches us that there are laws pertaining to the conservation of energy and matter. Energy is not a finite resource. When we look beyond our own world, we can see that we are constantly receiving more energy than we could ever think of depleting. When we worry and fear that there is not enough, all we are doing is squinting at the Universe and limiting the flow of abundant energy. However, even though our eyes are closed, the light does not go away. It is only in our ignorance that we think that there is darkness.

By living life in balance and in harmony with nature, there will be no shortages. By living in balance with each other, there will be no shortages. We need not worry if there is enough. This does not mean that some will not have more than others. Some plants grow bigger and produce more fruit. But it does mean that no one needs to go without.

Can this planet support an ever increasing population? Is there not only so much water? Are not tillable lands limited? We live in a somewhat closed system with respect to natural resources. It is also true that nature balances itself if inputs and outputs are not relatively equal. We all know the result of over-grazing, issues arising from population explosions and the role that diseases play in keeping systems in check. Overpopulation can become an issue.

Until such time as we evolve to the point that we can simply manifest basic needs by sheer thought, this is an area for caution. It is possible that excessive strains on resources could possibly stimulate new technologies to deal with the problem. It is usually through pressure that we rise to solve pressing issues.

"Therefore take no thought, saying, What shall we eat? or, What shall we drink? or, Wherewithal shall we be clothed? (For after all these things do the Gentiles seek) for your heavenly Father knoweth that ye have need of all these things."

Take no thought! In the movie "The Last Samurai" there is the admonishment to the American who is trying to learn the ancient ways of the sword (and failing miserably) that he is thinking too much. His thoughts are getting in the way of his performance and his intuition.

Yoda in the "Star Wars" films constantly tells Luke that he is also thinking too much and that he must give in to the "force." The Universe knows the needs of its own nature.

Within our own bodies, our cells do not worry. Water, proteins, vitamins and minerals are supplied to them on an as-needed basis. Within our subconscious mind is the mechanism that takes care of these needs, and the cells give no thought regarding how the building blocks of life are supplied.

In a way, we are cells in the cosmic body and the Cosmic Mind, the Universe, the Father/Mother knows what we require and has provided the resources necessary to meet those requirements.

Based upon the Law of Attraction, _worrying about how we shall be fed and clothed actually creates the illusion of lack._ By thinking that there is not enough to go around, we create a mental condition of "not enough to go around." We are all familiar with the notion of "worrying oneself ill." There are ample examples of those who never seem to have a "good break." While some may call it coincidence, there are numerous accounts of people who seem to attract what they fear most. Those who are concerned about their vehicle breaking down always seem to have car troubles. Those who worry about getting the flu always seem to get the flu. Those concerned about losing their jobs frequently lose their jobs. It is like the cartoon character with the dark cloud over his head that is exposed to all manner of personal disaster.

If form follows thought, especially those thoughts filled with deep-seated emotion, then the Law of Attraction goes to work and the fears, worries, and concerns become reality.

Conversely, there are those who go through life and nothing goes wrong. These people are confident of who and what they are and the saying, "the Midas touch," comes to mind. Faced with adverse circumstances, they come out ahead. Disasters become blessings. No problem is too big to tackle and each is addressed and corrected. Money is always available, health is good, the kids turn out great and abundance is observed in every aspect of their lives. I am not talking the rich and wealthy. I am not talking about heirs to financial kingdoms or empires. These are everyday people who just get it right. Their positive attitude in life attracts one blessing after another.

Many of these people have been born in the same circumstances as our "dark cloud" characters but through the use of will and determination have risen above adverse environmental and social influences. Many would say this is just good luck.

I do not think that Jesus was a believer in luck, nor do I think a mere series of circumstances separates the sheep from the goats. Do these people work hard? Have they furthered their education? Have they been in the right place at the right time? The answer is yes to these questions. Right thinking has conspired with them to create positive conditions that make all of these things possible. People like this live the Law of Attraction even if they have never heard of it.

It may be argued that these people are the exception to the rule. I would argue that if there are exceptions, then there is no rule. If one can do it, all can do it. The Universe knows what you need, and when positive thought is established as a habitual pattern, all of your needs and desires are met because the Universe goes into action. If you know that the Universe will take care of you, there is no need to take thought and worry about those things that are freely given when you are in a state of freely accepting.

CHAPTER SEVEN

How does a person achieve this state of knowing? How is it possible not to worry about the problems we may be facing today or those that may arise tomorrow? Critics would argue that you must plan for the future. Protect yourself from future financial perils or possible health issues. The notion of "live for today" is perhaps just a hippie holdover from the 60's that is dangerous and should be discarded. However, consider this. Perhaps the teachings of Jesus were, in fact, the basis of the rebellious culture that shook the West in the 60's and 70's.

"But seek ye first the kingdom of God, and his righteousness; and all these things shall be added unto you. Take therefore no thought for the morrow: for the morrow shall take thought for the things of itself. Sufficient unto the day is the evil thereof. Ask, and it shall be given you; seek, and ye shall find; knock, and it shall be opened unto you: for every one that asketh receiveth; and he that seeketh findeth; and to him that knocketh it shall be opened."

What is the Kingdom of God? Throughout the ages this phrase has been abused and misused. For many the Kingdom Of God is a place somewhere "up there." If, as many believe, God is omnipresent, or everywhere, then obviously there is no place that God is not. Jacob said whether I ascend to heaven or descend to hell, God is there. If this is true, the Kingdom of Heaven is as equally here as it is anywhere. The only reason we do not perceive it is because we are not aware of it in our conscious mind.

The Kingdom of Heaven is in each of us. It is not a place, but all places. It is not "out there," since it is everywhere. Jesus is telling us to become aware of the Kingdom of Heaven, to bring it into conscious awareness and then all that we desire will be made manifest.

All that we desire already exists in potential, we just need to accept the blessings and bring the potential into what we call reality. In this space, there is no need to "take thought." The Kingdom of Heaven is in, around and every place in between.

Awareness of the omnipresent Kingdom eliminates the need to worry about tomorrow and what the future may bring. This does not mean that it is wrong to be concerned with the future, but do not worry about it. The Universe will guide whatever action may be necessary to deal with tomorrow.

We all know that we often cross the proverbial bridge before we get there. We are so concerned that tomorrow may not be to our liking that we stress out over imagined events and often make ourselves ill. The illness often manifests in the form of heart disorder, stomach ulcers and even cancer. If we tell the Universe that we are worried about what may come, our message is for the Universe to bring more worry or to even manifest that which we worry about.

Jesus says to focus upon the present, the now, for sufficient are the evils today that we should address that which is before us, not what may come. When Jesus talks of evil, he is not saying that in the commonly presented way. By evil he is merely referring to the trials of everyday life.

When your consciousness is in the Kingdom of Heaven state, what is commonly referred to as "The Christ Consciousness," Ask and it shall be given you. This and the next few phrases are perhaps the most quoted with regards to the Law of Attraction. It is clear that Jesus did not say "plead, beg or demand and it shall be given unto you." When you are in "Christ consciousness," you merely ask and it shall be given to you.

The operative word here is conscious. Most of our lives we are not aware of our true estate. This does not mean that we are outside of the "Kingdom" for that is clearly impossible. What is happening is that we are unconsciously utilizing the Law of Attraction, but by not monitoring our thoughts, we attract both desirable and undesirable events.

An important way to look at this principle is to read it in the verse. What has been given unto you is what you have asked for. There is little doubt that few will ask for cancer, unemployment, rape, war, starvation, an auto accident or any of the myriad of tragedies that may befall humanity. Unfortunately, this is incorrect thinking. In some manner, shape or form, all that happens to you, you have created.

Perhaps a new Law or principle should be introduced, the **Law of Responsibility.** This law or principle states that each person is totally responsible for the all of the events that occur in their life. Most people do not want to hear this. It is easier to blame our social environment, our upbringing (or lack thereof), where we live, our teachers, our parents, some demonized enemy, the government, the police, the kids down the street, a mythical evil spirit, or even God Itself for all of our ills. It may be easier, but it is not true. We truly reap what we sow, spiritually, mentally, emotionally and physically.

"Seek and ye shall find." The Universe does place a burden upon us. It asks that we take action and seek the truth. While it would be nice if we could just sit and receive an influx of revelation or be struck with lightning like Saul, this happens to the few. It is not impossible, but few have the dedication to spend the time necessary to enter a life of contemplation. We have to search within our hearts and minds for that which we truly desire and not be distracted by other things.

When casually asked what we want from life the quick response is usually the new car, more money, fame, glory and a host of other desires that stem from our mass culture. There is nothing wrong with any of these things, and the Universe will provide if this is what we want. However, if this is what we most want most, don't be surprised if we then lack spiritual insight. Seek and ye shall find, but pay attention to exactly what it is you are seeking.

"Seeking" implies a quest in which we dig a bit deeper into our psyche to truly sort out the wheat from the chaff. It is not necessarily the things that we want, but rather the condition in our lives that the things may bring us. Money may give you a sense of security, peace of mind and freedom from worry. Thus, what is really sought is not the money but rather the sense of security and peace of mind.

Keep in mind that we do not need to tell the Universe how it will fulfill our desires. Simply express the heartfelt nature of those desires. The Universe may provide the money to fulfill our deepest hopes if it deems that is the best way to do so. However, it may not. Don't worry about how the gift is delivered or how it is wrapped. Rejoice in the gift. If you want money for a new home but the Universe just provides the home instead of the money, accept and rejoice.

Many go astray with the Law of Attraction by dictating to the Universe the way in which a wish is granted. In doing so, you place restrictions on all of the infinite ways wishes can be fulfilled and thereby restrict your own opportunities. It is the "forest for the trees" syndrome. An opportunity may be presented, but because your focus is on what you think is the best way to meet your desires, you pass up other options that may be even more beneficial.

Also note that with regard to seeking, the action required is not just mental. Seeking demands that you put into motion all of the resources at your disposal and take advantage of all the opportunities presented. If you seek that perfect soul mate, you will not find him or her by staying stuck in your home. You have to get out in order to "meet" the opportunities.

Similarly, if you seek the perfect job, it is incumbent upon you to check the want ads and talk or write to others about your desires. The job of the Universe is to set the energies in motion; it is up to you to be in the right place at the right time.

If wealth is sought and you suddenly get an idea for a new business, a new employment opportunity or are asked to join a group or organization, this may be the way the Universe is acting to help you find what you desire.

Remember also the Law of Responsibility. What you find in your life, in some way you have brought into manifestation. If you do not like what you find, it is your responsibility to seek again. This is not a ball game. It is not three strikes and you are out. The game of life has no set quarters or time limits. There is no fourth down where you are forced to punt. Your opportunities are endless, regardless of what you have been told and despite appearances to the contrary.

"Knock, and it shall be opened up to you." Once again, we are asked to take action. Almost every waking moment, we are faced with choices or doors that we either choose to enter or pass by. Many go through life entering and exiting doors that are controlled by others. Little thought is given as to the nature of the door and where it may lead. Like the old time carnivals, we are told to "step right in for the thrill of a lifetime." It is sad how many succumb to this entreaty.

Those who are successful in life choose the doors upon which they knock. If the experience in the place they enter is negative, they do not view it as a mistake. Rather, they view it as an opportunity to better determine which door they will knock on next. Remember, the places you have entered have been your choice. Knowingly or unknowingly, you have knocked upon that door and, without judgment, the door was opened unto you.

The formula presented by Jesus seems very simple. Ask and you receive, seek and you will find, knock and the door is opened. Out of context, the formula is simple but it must be remembered that other "conditions" apply. Too many have sought to present the Laws of Attraction and Responsibility in this simple way. The non-believers are perhaps rightly justified in their skepticism. They can point to many examples where this prescription for success has failed and thereby reject the entire concept. The key is to keep in mind the context. You must come from a place of no judgment; you must be in the light and have clarity of thought. You must be in the Kingdom. There can be no doubt or worry, and you must see the fields already white with the harvest in order for the process to work.

These and several other key principles provide the context for attracting and manifesting your "new earth" and your "new heaven."

CHAPTER EIGHT

The casual experimenter will probably have little success with the Law of Attraction and the process that is outlined by Jesus in these pages. If you enter this process with an attitude of, "I guess it will not hurt to try it," then you might as well seek some other means to fulfill your desires.

"No man putteth a piece of new cloth upon an old garment; else the new piece that filleth it up agreeth not with the old: it taketh away from the old, and the rent is made worse.

Another parable put he forth.

And no man putteth new wine into old bottles; else the bottles will be marred: the new wine will burst the bottles, and be spilled, and the bottles shall perish. But new wine must be put into new bottles; and both are preserved..."

If the inner person is not changed, these new ideas could only make matters worse. The "new cloth" is the new idea that you can change your reality and manifest your heart's desire. The old garment is your current state of mind, the way you view the world and the extent to which you can accept a reversal in your thinking. If you cannot repent, if you cannot change your mind, the new ideas will only serve to cause you frustration and disappointment. This will make the "rent," or tear, worse in the mindset in which you are clothed. This could lead to a focus upon the negative and as a result you will attract more of what you do not want or desire. These types of cautions are frequently neglected and cause many to doubt the efficacy of the ideas.

The "new wine" in the old bottle can burst the very fabric of your thought system. This can sour your general outlook on life and lead you down the road of further desperation. You must put new wine into "new bottles." In this, you alter your fundamental way of thinking and you are, in a sense, "born again" into a new way of thinking and a new outlook on life.

While this process is not that difficult, it does require focus and attention on the way you think and your reaction to the events that occur in your life. As the bottle becomes new, it can accept more wine. However, the steps in this process are fairly precise and to attempt shortcuts will result in failure.

Failure is not as negative as the word implies. It is by learning from our failures that we grow and evolve. Like I said, you are not on a pre-set time frame. As far as the Universe is concerned, you have eternity to create your new bottle. It is you who creates a sense of urgency and all of the stress that goes along with your concern for tomorrow.

CHAPTER NINE

If we are filled with doubt and lack surety, our efforts at determining our own destiny will crumble. If our intention is uncertain, then our mind is divided and that which we are trying to build cannot stand.

"And if a kingdom be divided against itself, that kingdom cannot stand. And if a house be divided against itself, that house cannot stand. And if Satan rise up against himself, and be divided, he cannot stand, but hath an end.

No man can enter into a strong man's house, and spoil his goods, except he will first bind the strong man; and then he will spoil his house."

Each of you is the Kingdom. The way you think, act and view the world is your kingdom. It is your reality and, for better or worse, you have created it. If your thoughts are divided and you perceive any attempt at altering your life with skepticism, your mental house will collapse. If Satan, or, more truthfully, temptation, convinces you to buy into appearances, sends you mixed messages about the probability of actually altering your life, your thought process will not stand and your effort will come to an end.

Appearances are deceiving and when we give into appearance and illusion, we see pain, suffering and lack. These things are real, but they are not "actual." Our fundamental state of energy suffers no pain and lacks for nothing. When we take that energy and form it into a picture that is not pleasing, we have only altered appearance, we have not altered the basic nature of energy.

The strong man is the appearance. We have put our faith and trust into our five senses and yet science will tell you they are very deceiving. Things in a distance look small, and yet they are not. We hear only a very minor band of tones. We see but a fraction of the light waves that engulf our being. Our taste can be fooled by smell and our touch is altered by our perceptions. Despite all of this, we are told that "seeing is believing." The mystics would say, "What we believe is what we see" or "As above in consciousness, so below in matter."

So the strong man or the world of illusion impinges upon our ability to see the truth. This strong man may bind our thoughts to these appearances and, if we accept the illusion as truth, he will destroy our house. This strong man is not some sentient being that we have all demonized in order to justify our lack of willingness to take responsibility for our lives. The senses are wonderful things when we use them with understanding and knowledge, but they do not tell the entire picture.

CHAPTER TEN

Is wealth something to be shunned? Is it something evil? We are not here to be poor, sick, or lonely.

"But woe unto you that are rich! For ye have received your consolation."

"Woe unto you that are full! For ye shall hunger."

A first reading of these lines would imply that it is not in your best interests to have wealth and comforts. At least, that is what religious leaders would have you believe. And yet, those same leaders collect your tithes and many seem a bit on the plump side. My interpretation is a little different. There are those in life who believe that wealth is an end, rather than a means to achieve a greater good. There are also those who are so full of themselves they think they know it all, they keep all that they have just for themselves and, for fear of loss, share not with others.

These people shall hunger, not for food, but for meaning and purpose. These people shall leave this world with few friends and the spoils of their labor shall be divided amongst the heirs. While Jesus does not condemn wealth and material possessions, I believe that he does imply that care should be taken with how one uses such wealth. Those who believe that the Universe is limited in its bounty close themselves off from others, thinking what they have will be taken away. Often, this fear attracts the loss of such things.

But those who know that there are no limits give of their riches and bounty freely and it always seems that more comes their way.

"Judge not, and ye shall not be judged: condemn not, and ye shall not be condemned: forgive, and ye shall be forgiven."

Make no final decisions about the nature of the Universe. It changes constantly. Do not condemn others for what they have. The wealth of the Universe is available to all. With our condemnations, we attract that which we condemn. Thoughts filled with strong emotion and negative intentions only return to us. It is a Wiccan belief that negative thoughts are returned threefold. Negative energy does not exist. You cannot put a curse upon someone or cause harm with your thoughts or intentions. Black magic is a myth perpetuated by those who would keep you frightened like a little child. In this way they can get you to do all manner of things that go against your own inner voice. In truth, all you do is poison your own thoughts and what you condemn and fear becomes the guiding force in your life.

The idea of forgiveness can be difficult for many. If a person is caught in the trap of malice and hatred, these things are attracted to that person. Bitterness never turns sweet and the joys of life become as a sour fruit. It is almost impossible to enter the "kingdom" or Christ consciousness if hatred is still held within the heart and mind.

There is no question that abuse is hard to forgive. Murder is hard to forgive. The loss of a loved one to a drunk driver is hard to forgive. War is hard to forgive. However, unless the cycle of condemnation is broken, it continues to perpetuate itself. Is this the reason why some parts of the world are never at peace?

When we forgive others, we are forgiven. It is not that some god forgives you, it is you that forgives you. What good is it for deity to forgive if you do not? How can we be admonished not to judge, condemn and to forgive and then think that God would not automatically do these things?

This is a message to each of you. It is you that must move on and perhaps look for the inner meaning of those negative things that may have happened. It is you who must discover that ever so elusive blessing in that awfully dark cloud. When this is done, all manner of illnesses disappear and you can move to partake of the riches that await.

"Give, and it shall be given unto you; good measure, pressed down, and shaken together, and running over, shall men give into your bosom. For with the same measure that ye mete withal it shall be measured to you again."

What you put into your life, your thoughts and your emotions will be returned unto you. *This IS the Law of Attraction and the Law of Responsibility at work.* Who does the giving back? What you send out with the power of thought, filled with emotion and strong intention, the Universe will return back to you in "good measure, pressed down" and made manifest in your life. We all use the phrase, "what goes around, comes around." This applies for both positive and negative thoughts. My guess is that this is the genesis of that common saying.

The way you measure and think about the world, your life, your friends, your family, your lot in life, your health, your desires, hopes and dreams will be measured back to you. If you want to know how you view the world, simply look at what is in your life, for it is a mirror of your deepest thoughts.

Many are surprised when they actually stop to look and then realize that their life is a product of their own mind. Remember, the doors that have been opened are the ones you opened. If you do not like what you see, you can change your measure. You can view things in a different way and alter what is measured back.

There is no reason for any sense of guilt if what you see is not how you wish your life to be. It only means that you need to alter your perceptions. We often learn through the negative. In other words, we discover who we are by discovering what we are not. If something negative is manifest in your life you can say, "That is not me, it is not the way I want to be."

With this change of mindset, your world will begin to adjust to your new thought patterns. If you buy a book or go to a movie and do not like it, there is no reason for any sense of guilt. You simply move on and don't buy more of the same kinds of books and do not see similar movies. And yet, each book or movie you do not like teaches you more about yourself and about what you do or do not want to be. This means that even these negative experiences can become a positive force in your life.

CHAPTER ELEVEN

Our deepest thoughts and desires are expressed outwardly as our physical reality. A person's actions, the way they live and the way they treat and speak of others and the way that they respond to the world is a reflection of their inner thoughts.

"For a good tree bringeth not forth corrupt fruit; neither doth a corrupt tree bring forth good fruit. For every tree is known by his own fruit. For of thorns men do not gather figs, nor of a bramble bush gather they grapes."

You cannot hide from yourself since the outer is a mirror of the inner. Those who are gentle of heart and of positive intention bring forth these attributes in every aspect of their lives. Regardless of what circumstances may befall them, their outer world still reflect inner calm and peace. It is not that everyone "walks their talk," but they do "walk their thoughts."

We all create our own outer reality even if we do not "see" that we are responsible for what is imaged in our outer world.

We have all experienced hypocrisy. We have all known people who proclaim love and forgiveness with one hand as they use the other hand to hate and seek revenge. This is evident at the individual level and the collective level in terms of nations. Grapes do not grow on the bramble bush and those who attempt to hide their negative thoughts in the guise of sweet sounding platitudes are known by their corrupt fruit.

What is a key principle here is that our manifest world is the result of the nature of the "tree," the heartwood, the thoughts and true values within. We are responsible for the fruit that we bare, for our fruits are the product of who and what we really are at any particular moment of creation.

If disease is in our life, we need to examine what is within that gives rise to the corrupt fruit. If we lack material comforts, what thoughts or emotions within give rise to those brambles? If we find it difficult to attract friends and a life partner, what intentions give rise to the thorns? We cannot blame someone else or a social or environmental condition for the quality of our fruit. A strong and healthy plant is not susceptible to the ravages of disease, insect or changes in weather. They stand tall against adversity and it is their inner strength that sees them through setbacks.

This is also true of people. The quality of our fruit is not a condemnation nor is it a reason to feel guilt or shame. They are simply signposts, indicators that our inner thoughts require tending and perhaps some loving attention in order to improve the quality of the harvest.

"A good man out of the good treasure of his heart bringeth forth that which is good; and an evil man out of the evil treasure of his heart bringeth forth that which is evil: for of the abundance of the heart his mouth speaketh."

I am not a believer in the Biblical notion of "good and evil." I believe those terms were used by many since those were the public terms or common vernacular of the day. The more appropriate terms are positive and negative as they are the words of choice among the mystics and they more accurately represent the true concept. Good and evil imply opposing forces that struggle with each other for dominance and also some intelligent force of evil that competes with an intelligent force of good. This is simply not the case.

Positive and negative forces are the dualities that make the manifest world possible. Hot and cold, up and down, front and back, light and dark are but a few examples of that duality in which the existence of one is dependent upon the other.

People think and act both positively and negatively. Each term, however is relative and each a degree of the other. As mentioned, we make no final decision about the polarity of an event since oftentimes the perceived negative turns out to be positive, and vice versa. After all, down is not "bad" if your plane is running out of fuel. Up is not necessarily good to a mouse that wants to keep all fours on the ground. All positives and negatives are relative and often subjective.

All of that being said, the meaning of this saying is rather clear in that we are told that what is inside becomes pictured outside. Our reality reflects those things that garner intense emotional support. These can either be positive or negative energies that form the basis of our home, work and social environments. The "good" treasure is pictured as a world with positive events and relationships. The "evil" or negative treasure creates the broken families, child abuse, loss of employment, minimal friendships and strained relationships.

It is important to mention that emphasis is also placed on the power of speech. Speech is a sound, which in turn is a vibration. *When emotions, the positive or negative treasures of the heart, are released verbally, more energy is put into the treasures.*

Many inspirational speakers and writers will point out the importance of verbalizing your positive intentions in order to manifest your desires. We live in a material world and sound is a vibration that affects that world. Sounds can make us feel happy or sad, irritable, pleasant, sleepy or excited. When inner thoughts and emotions are released as words, more power is given to that vibration and its effect is greater. Saying, "I love you" has more meaning and impact than just thinking it, as does expressing feelings of hatred. Warriors have often used the beating of drums, chants, and shouts to build courage and to frighten the opponent. Music has also been used to stir pride and devotion to nations, as well as bringing tears to the eyes in remembrance of lost loves and tragedies.

Sound, in the form of speech, is a very powerful tool. When thoughts are released into the physical world, the Universe is more fully convinced that what you are thinking is what you want to manifest. When thought plus emotion plus sound is released on the physical plane, the chances of manifestation are increased. The wise have often cautioned of keeping silent or at least thinking before speaking. A thought that is released on the physical plane in the form of words can have either positive or negative effects, so the prudent will choose their words carefully.

"He is like a man which built an house, and digged deep, and laid the foundation on a rock: and when the flood arose, the stream beat vehemently upon that house, and could not shake it: for it was founded upon a rock. But he that heareth and doeth not, is like a man that without a foundation built an house upon the earth; against which the stream did beat vehemently, and immediately it fell; and the ruin of that house was great."

Our ideas and concepts of the Universe and the world in which we live is our mental house. If it is built on the solid rock of understanding, knowledge and experience, then it is built on solid ground. This type of mental house can withstand the onslaught of negative thinking.

Water is esoterically the same as one's stream of consciousness. When built on rock, the flow of ideas from the ignorant does not weaken or shake one's mental house. When all those around you claim that we live in a horrible world and that the way people think cannot change anything, the house on the stone withstands this mental and emotional attack and rejects those ideas as nonsense.

It is difficult to have convictions that are founded upon solid ground. The world is changing rapidly and few are able to keep their footing in the raging torrent of negative thinking. As a result, many a house is swept away and becomes ruled by fear, despair, confusion, mistrust and hatred. It becomes easy to demonize a country, an ethnic group or race and to lay fault upon their shoulders for our misgivings. It becomes easy not to take up the mantle of personal responsibility and to lay blame at the feet of others.

And yet, this very act of turning responsibility over to others is, in fact, a choice for which we are responsible. The Law of Responsibility cannot be given away, despite appearances to the contrary.

CHAPTER TWELVE

Jesus did not limit his comments to religious thought. While many would have you think that all that he said was about the church, which did not even exist, Jesus was speaking about life.

"Go thy way; and as thou hast believed, so be it done unto thee."

This quote should be emblazoned into your heart and mind. Jesus made this as a statement of fact. He did not use words like "maybe," "possibly," "wouldn't it be nice," or "if's and buts". This is a definitive statement:, "as you believe, it is done to you." He made no reference that this was limited to spiritual or religious matters. He made no suggestion that it only pertained to church, politics, family, culture, customs, relationships, education or any other singular aspect of life. What you believe is what you get. He did not imply "that seeing is believing" but clearly says that believing is seeing. What you believe becomes your world. What you believe becomes your reality in every facet of your life.

Buddha said, **"We are what we think. With our thoughts we make the world."** I think Buddha and Jesus would have been good friends. This has been the message of every great avatar, and it is one that is often overlooked and ignored in the pulpits. The foundation of our world and the reality we live in emerges from our individual and collective thought patterns.

To all, this belief should be a joyous revelation. No longer are you loosely chained to the pillar of ignorance. In the Tarot, card number 15 is the Devil. On this card we see what some have called Satan on a block. He is grotesque, with the head of a goat, wings, clawed feet and he is crowned with an inverted pentagram. At his feet are a naked man and a woman with chains around their necks. Many misinterpret this card and say that humanity is tied to the devil.

Closer examination reveals that the chains around the neck of the figures are very loose and can be easily removed. The chains are the illusion. The chains are for those who think that we do not control our reality. The wise know that the chains can be easily thrown off. The pentagram is a symbol that speaks to humanity's divinity. Four points are the four elements and the fifth represents the human spirit.

When enclosed in a circle, its simple meaning is that man has dominance over the elements, reality. All are enclosed in the circle of the Universe. In the Devil card, the star is inverted or upside down and the circle is missing. The meaning is that man, in his ignorance, has forgotten his relationship to the Universe and that rather than controlling the elements, a.k.a. his reality, he is controlled by them.

This is the myth and the Great Illusion that has been kept from common knowledge and thought for so many years. The myth is the yoke or the chains around our neck.

"GO THY WAY!" Jesus did not say to follow the ways of others. He did not say to let others determine the way you think or believe. He did not say let others create your reality. _This is your life,_ go your way and your beliefs will create the world and the reality you desire. You are to take full responsibility for your life. Do not give it away to others. Do not accept the chains of erroneous beliefs. You are responsible for what you think and what you believe and what you create.

"For whosoever hath, to him shall be given, and he shall have more abundance: but whosoever hath not, from him shall be taken away even that he hath."

Whatever you have, whatever you hold in your beliefs and thoughts, are given unto you. If your thoughts and beliefs are filled with abundance, you will have more abundance. If you believe in lack and scarcity, the little you have will be taken away because you believe that they will or can be taken away. **This is the Law of Abundance.**

The question is do you want abundance in a positive way or a negative way? You can create an abundance of not having as easily as an abundance of having. Again, there is no restriction on the type of abundance you can create. Jesus does not qualify his statement and say you can only have spiritual abundance. There are people that just cannot seem to get a break and then there are those who can do no wrong. Those that do not get the breaks have a belief that they will not get one and that the world is out to take what they have. This belief is made manifest.

Remember that there is no judgment involved here. There is no deity saying that only the faithful to a particular dogma or creed will get what they want. At the time of Jesus there was no dogma or creed. This is why it is said that the Universe is objective and that it is "no respecter of persons." It does not matter to what religion you belong. The Laws work regardless. No one is singled out for special favor or dispensation. All have equal access to the abundance of the Universe. The only limits are those placed by your beliefs.

"For there is nothing hid, neither was any thing kept secret, which shall not be manifested; but that it should be known and come abroad."

Anything and everything held in the subconscious and conscious mind is manifested. If these thoughts are imbued with powerful emotion and intention, they are made manifest and are made known. Nothing is hidden nor kept secret. You are what you think and your reality is made known as your beliefs are made manifest.

You may argue that this is out of context but if you follow the stream of the thoughts of Jesus you will see that this is not the case. He continuously states that your thinking is your reality. Obviously, passing thoughts and ideas that hold no deep-seated energy do not emerge. But it is obvious that strong thoughts are brought into reality in some manner. This includes illness. Nothing is hidden. Somewhere in your mind there is a belief that you will or are experiencing disease. Somewhere in your mind is the idea that you will not be prosperous or that you will live a lonely life. Nothing is hidden. All will be made known by the things and events that appear in your life. Your thoughts and your reality are one.

"Take heed what ye hear: with what measure ye mete, it shall be measured to you: and unto you that hear shall more be given: for he that hath, to him shall be given: and he that hath not, from him shall be taken even that which he hath."

Be careful what you allow to enter your mind. This does not mean to close your ears to the world around you. But it does mean that you should take care what you believe that others say. Always question the news. Always question others' beliefs and dogma, because what you accept becomes your new reality. When you hear what you believe to be the truth, more truth will come your way. When you decide that a certain way of life is best suited for you, more of that life will arrive on your doorstep.

When you decide that drug use is not for you, those who take drugs will fade from your life. When you decide that there are no limits to the abundance of the Universe, more is given to you. When you decide that you would like to embark upon a new path, suddenly you have company and new friends appear. If you accept the political notion that a particular county or people are evil, they will become evil to you.

It is incumbent upon you to filter what others say and do not believe all that is said. Be careful what you accept as truth and allow only those words that ring true to enter your mind and your life. As we must be careful as to the vibrations that we send out with our words, so must we be careful as to what vibrations we allow to take root in our minds.

CHAPTER THIRTEEN

"Be not afraid, only believe. Fear not: believe only, and she shall be made whole. According to your faith be it unto you."

Healing is a matter of belief. This is so difficult for so many to accept. Know the truth and the truth shall be made manifest in your life. Can we bring a loved one back from the dead? At this stage in our evolution this is probably not possible. And besides, all things travel the great circle of life in cycles, there is truly a time to each season. But, if we recognize that somewhere deep inside we are the cause of our own ailments, it is possible to rid ourselves of disease.

We have all heard stories of miraculous recoveries from pain and disease. Studies have shown that those with a positive and knowing outlook on life get through life-threatening ailments better and quicker than those whose minds are filled with defeat. According to what you believe, it is done to you. "Take up thy bed", and with a new set of beliefs and a new way of thinking, very little is impossible.

CHAPTER FOURTEEN

In describing the Kingdom of Heaven Jesus spoke in parables. He made comparisons that most would understand since it is almost impossible to put into words that which is a state of mind and heart. Jesus did not describe a physical place; he described a state of mind. This would make sense since he earlier proclaimed that the kingdom of heaven is here, now, and available to all who wish to enter. It is but a thought away.

"Whereunto shall we liken the kingdom of God? Or with what comparison shall we compare it? A grain of mustard seed is the least of all seeds: is indeed less than all the seeds that be in the earth; but when it is sown in the earth, it groweth up: it becometh greater than all herbs; it shooteth out great branches, and becometh a tree, so that the fowls of the air come and lodge in the branches thereof."

The kingdom of heaven is like unto leaven, which a woman took, and hid in three measures of meal, till the whole was leavened.

You have heard it a thousand times— the kingdom of heaven is within you. When given the opportunity, it grows from the smallest seed of truth and provides a home for all of your thoughts, hopes and desires. It is the small fragment of yeast that gives rise to the bread that nourishes our life.

"All these things spake Jesus unto the multitude in parables."

Then Jesus sent the multitude away, and went into the house and his disciples came unto him, saying, declare unto us the parable of the tares of the field. He answered,

"He that soweth the good seed is the Son of man; the field is the world; the good seed are the children of the kingdom; but the tares are the children of the wicked one; the enemy that sowed them is the devil; the harvest is the end of the world; and the reapers are the angels.

As therefore the tares are gathered and burned in the fire; so shall it be in the end of this world. The Son of man shall send forth his angels, and they shall gather out of his kingdom all things that offend, and them which do iniquity; and shall cast them into a furnace of fire: there shall be wailing and gnashing of teeth."

He that sows is all of us. *The field is our minds*. The good seeds are the thoughts of truth and understanding. The tares are our negative thoughts. Illusion sowed the negative thoughts. The harvest is the end of pain, suffering and want that is the end of the world as you have known it. The reapers are purified thoughts.

The negative thoughts are sent to the fire of transmutation—truth. It is then that our negative thoughts cease to exist. Our mind will resist this journey toward enlightenment and they will attempt to keep us in our old mold of thinking.

"Again, the kingdom of heaven is like unto treasure hid in a field; which when a man hath found, he hideth, and for joy thereof goeth and selleth all that he hath, and buyeth that field."

The treasure in the field is the light within, the truth, that which connects you to the infinite power of the Universe. When you find that truth that rests at the center of your being, little else matters. This is why so many forget that the Law of Attraction is not just about fame and fortune. It is about finding the true nature of your being that denies you nothing and gives you everything.

"Again, the kingdom of heaven is like unto a merchant man, seeking goodly pearls: who, when he had found one pearl of great price, went and sold all that he had, and bought it."

Is it not better to have one thing of great value than many things of no value? To know the perfection within is to release that perfection into the world. It is letting your light shine and allowing the inner and the outer to be as one.

"Again, the kingdom of heaven is like unto a net, that was cast into the sea, and gathered of every kind: which, when it was full, they drew to shore, and sat down, and gathered the good into vessels, but cast the bad away."

It is said, _"Garbage in, garbage out."_ So many accept mediocrity and thereby have a mediocre life. Most feel that they have to accept the "good with the bad." However, the fact is there is no need to accept any bad. Your cup can overflow with the positive. We are exposed to a constant barrage of ideas and images, but it is not necessary to accept them all as gospel. Each concept must be examined in the light of our inner being and inner truths. That which rings true can be accepted and taken into vessels, or the mind. That which is deemed inappropriate should be cast away.

"Hearken unto me every one of you. Hear and understand. Not that which goeth into the mouth defileth a man; but that which

cometh out of the mouth, this defileth a man. There is nothing from without a man that entering into him can defile him: but the things which come out of him, those are they that defile the man."

Jesus is fairly adamant on this point. He is saying, "Hey, pay attention, I have something important to tell you." What goes into the body cannot defile the body. What goes into the mind cannot defile the mind. What goes into the heart cannot defile the heart. It is always what you do with what you see and hear that matters. Nothing outside of you can hurt you unless you let it hurt you. It is only the thoughts and emotions and words and intentions that you express which can cause you any harm.

You are your own world and you are the master of that world. No one can hurt you. Nothing can cripple you. Nothing can cause you pain or suffering unless YOU allow it to be part of your reality.

"Are ye also yet so without understanding? Do not ye yet perceive that whatsoever thing from without entereth into a man, entereth in at the mouth, goeth into the belly, and is cast out into the draught, purging all meats? It entereth not into his heart; it cannot defile him."

I think that the Master was getting a little impatient at this point. Negative thoughts and ideas that assault your senses need not be a part of your world. You can take these things in, but they can just as easily be expelled as nitrogenous waste. _If the things that you consume do not enter your heart and do not become part of your being, they CANNOT harm you._

This does not mean that you become blind to the troubles in the world around you; but, it does mean that you can see the truth of every situation.

The power that Jesus used to heal the blind and the sick was not some mysterious form of magic. *He healed with his vision.* He refused to accept blindness and disease into his reality and so they ceased to have any existence. The sheer clarity of his vision was transferred to the blind man and thus sight was returned. In fact, it was never really gone. The blind man accepted the bad fish and thus they were a part of his world.

This does not have to be the case. We do not have to accept pain, suffering, poverty or disease. When we see from the perspective of our inner light, we see all things whole, all people fed and consequently all sadness fades as a distant memory.

"But those things which proceed out of the mouth come forth from the heart; and they defile the man: for from within, out of the heart of men, proceed evil thoughts, adulteries, fornications, murders, thefts, covetousness, wickedness, deceit, lasciviousness, an evil eye, blasphemy, pride, foolishness: all these evil things come from within, and these are the things which defile a man: but to eat with unwashen hands defileth not a man."

There is a distinction between *KNOWLEDGE and KNOWING.* Knowledge is the accumulation of information. Knowing is the inner understanding of that information. Knowing separates truth from fiction. Here is a KEY regarding the Law of Attraction. Many people have information, knowledge, regarding spiritual laws. They can cite chapter and verse, list the steps to be followed, proclaim the grandest of truths, but, when push comes to shove, do not have a clue what it all really means.

The secret to the utilization of any law is the knowing of the inner meaning. It comes from the heart that knows and sees and believes in the truth of its nature. If your beliefs are false, your world is false. If your beliefs are true, your world is true. If you believe that the man is blind, he will, in your reality, remain blind. Negative thoughts come from within. When expressed, they defile your life. They create the illusion.

"All these evil things come from within." There is _no exterior evil force in the world._ All evil, negativity, comes from within and is expressed as hatred, murder, violence, disease and all the ills that we have been able to imagine or have been told has existence. When negative thoughts leave our minds they take on an expression in the outer world, in our reality. Usually, they will take the form of that which we most fear. To eat with "unwashen hands," or, rather, to live in a world filled with negative ideas, does not defile a man. It is only when we accept the reality as truth and we in turn espouse that false truth that it becomes a part of our reality.

CHAPTER FIFTEEN

It is here that an esoteric principle must be clarified. _There is a difference between reality and actuality._ Reality is the outer appearance that is perceived by the senses. Actuality is the true nature of a thing or the Universe or a situation. A red shirt is "really" red, but it is actually every color but red. It looks really red because the fabric does not absorb the red wavelength and it is reflected to the eyes. All other colors have been absorbed by the shirt except red. Thus, the shirt is really red, but it is not actually red.

Our senses only perceive a very small fraction of the world in which we live. Most think that light is white and yet it is comprised of the rainbow. Most do not realize that radio waves, X-rays, gamma waves and more are also light. A pitch dark room with a radio playing is filled with light. It is really dark, but it is actually filled with light.

"Every plant, which my heavenly Father hath not planted, shall be rooted up. Let them alone: they be blind leaders of the blind. And if the blind lead the blind, both shall fall into the ditch."

Every plant is every thought, idea or concept that is not actual. Reality is the illusion that will dissolve and be uprooted when the mind awakens to the true nature of the Universe. Death, disease, poverty and loneliness are real, but they are not actual. Those who think that they are poor have untold riches in the Universal bank. Those that are ill need but see with true vision to discover that illness is a mirage or a mask. Those who proclaim the world to be evil can only live in an evil world. They are the blind that have led humanity through the millennia. They are the blind who have taken their followers into the ditch.

"If thou canst because of your unbelief: for verily I say unto you, If ye have faith as a grain of mustard seed, ye shall say unto this mountain, Remove hence to yonder place; and it shall remove; and nothing shall be impossible unto you."

If you "know" the true power that lies within, nothing is impossible. The only stumbling block to performing every conceivable miracle is the lack of knowing or believing that all things are possible. Moving mountains, ending poverty, achieving world peace and more are only a thought away.

"...believe, all things are possible to him that believeth."

All things are possible, no exceptions. Jesus did not say you had to believe in a certain god or attend church, or be of a particular race or ethnicity, just believe and all of your desires are made manifest. Believe and all things are attracted unto you in overflowing abundance. There are no limits. There is no mountain that cannot be climbed, no disease that cannot be cured, no situation that cannot be changed, no relationship that cannot be found, no desire that cannot be made manifest.

In this context, the term belief is not to be confused with the idea of "hope." Hoping is just wishful thinking. Belief must be viewed as knowing. Know that these words are true and all things ARE possible. Know that the kingdom and the power are within you. Know that nothing outside of you, nothing outside of your reality, can hurt you. Know that your new vision and your new hearing will enable you to attract all that you desire. Know that you do not have to wait for months for the harvest. The fields are NOW white and ready to be gleaned. There is no waiting! There is nothing that you cannot achieve or have. ALL things are possible RIGHT NOW!

"Judge not according to the appearance, but judge righteous judgment."

Make no final decisions according to what you see. Do not rely upon the senses to give you a true understanding of the world. Look within to discover the true nature about the world in which you live. All things are possible if you see with the inner vision. See the harvest where others see none. See abundance where others see only poverty. See wholeness where others see disease. See love where others see hatred. See solutions where others see problems. See strength where others see weakness. See success where others see failure. See beginnings where others see endings. See open where others see closed. This is righteous judgment.

CHAPTER SIXTEEN

"Is it not written in your law, I said, Ye are gods?"

While Jesus did not say you are God, the implication should be obvious. It is in this simple line that the Master sums up the power available to everyone. We all possess the creative power of the Universe. We all have the ability to create the reality we desire.

Is this liberty to do whatever we want both positive and negative? Does this give us the freedom to do harm unto others? Does this give us the right to abuse the creative power and to become selfish and greedy?

No, this is not a license for humanity to run rampart through life in a destructive manner. That is why it is so important to follow Jesus' stream of thought. When one operates from the kingdom within and from the light, it is discovered that the creative forces of the Universe can only be used in a positive way.

It is only in our forgetfulness of our relationship to all of the threads of life that we become servants of the illusion, rather than its master.

"If a son shall ask bread of any of you that is a father, will he give him a stone? Or if he ask a fish, will he for a fish give him a serpent? Or if he shall ask an egg, will he offer him a scorpion?"

The stones, the serpent and the scorpion are of our own creation. A father does not wish ill upon his son. A father does not demand sacrifice. A father does not require worship, or poverty, or suffering, pain or sorrow. Nowhere are these demanded. No parent requires these things of their children. A GOD would never require the lament of its offspring, and yet so many have been convinced that this is the case. So many have been taught and believe that a father would create an evil demon to constantly torment his children. This is not the God of Jesus and it is not the god that Jesus says that you each are.

"If ye then, being evil, know how to give good gifts unto your children: how much more shall your heavenly Father give the Holy Spirit to them that ask him"

There is no true evil, just true ignorance. But in our ignorance, we still give all that we can to our children. We make whatever sacrifice is necessary to ensure that their life is a better life. Would any real God do less? If you love your children, how much more does God love his children? If you want only the best for your sons and daughters, how much more does God want this for you?

"Therefore I say unto you, Take no thought for your life, what ye shall eat; neither for the body, what ye shall put on. The life is more than meat, and the body is more than raiment."

"Consider the ravens: for they neither sow nor reap; which neither have storehouse nor barn; and God feedeth them: how much more are ye better than the fowls?"

"And which of you with taking thought can add to his stature one cubit? If ye then be not able to do that thing which is least, why take ye thought for the rest?"

"Consider the lilies how they grow: they toil not, they spin not; and yet I say unto you, that Solomon in all his glory was not

arrayed like one of these. If then God so clothe the grass, which is to day in the field, and to morrow is cast into the oven; how much more will he clothe you, O ye of little faith?"

"And seek not ye what ye shall eat, or what ye shall drink, neither be ye of doubtful mind. For all these things do the nations of the world seek after: and your Father knoweth that ye have need of these things."

"But rather seek ye the kingdom of God; and all these things shall be added unto you".

These are but a restating of what has been revealed, but it is important to note the frequency with which the keys are given and the rarity with which they are used. Seek that which is the truth within and all of your needs and desires will be met. Remove the blinders and see that all that you could ever want has already been delivered.

"Fear not, little flock; for it is your Father's good pleasure to give you the kingdom. Sell that ye have, and give alms; provide yourselves bags which wax not old, a treasure in the heavens that faileth not, where no thief approacheth, neither moth corrupteth. For where your treasure is, there will your heart be also."

It is the will of the Universe that all your desires be fulfilled. If you build your mental foundation on the solid rock of knowing, then no illusion, no thief, no false ideas can ever take away what you have created. When you knowingly take responsibility for your thoughts, actions and words, you are on a foundation of stone.

Understand that your needs are already met. The treasure in heaven is the treasure that you find in your heart and mind. It is only when we believe that others are in control or that we have no responsibility for our lives that the moths enter and corrupt or blind us from the truth of existence.

"Blessed are those servants, whom the lord when he cometh shall find watching: verily I say unto you, that he shall gird himself, and make them to sit down to meat, and will come forth and serve them. And if he shall come in the second watch, or come in the third watch, and find them so, blessed are those servants. And this know, that if the goodman of the house had known what hour the thief would come, he would have watched, and not have suffered his house to be broken through. Be ye therefore ready also: for the Son of man cometh at an hour when ye think not."

This is not about a "second coming" in the sense that has been promoted in religious dogma. This is not a threat about being good and loyal church followers because you never know when God may come and pass judgment. If that were the case, it would contradict all that has been previously said. I do not believe that Jesus was unaware of what he taught from day to day.

This is about the necessity to always monitor your thoughts and emotions. You never know when you may be confronted by what may appear to be something negative. You never know when your thoughts may be taken by surprise by worldly or personal events or circumstances. One must always be aware of one's emotions and thought patterns. Since form follows thought, it is easy to make slight shifts in your reality and personal life if your thoughts are not properly tended.

A good gardener always keeps an eye out for weeds and predators that may cause damage to the crop. We must all be good mental gardeners. We must all be open for new inspirations and new ideas or, in old terms, for the coming of the Son of man.

"Children, how hard is it for them that trust in riches to enter into the kingdom of God! Verily I say unto you, That a rich man shall hardly enter into the kingdom of heaven! And again I say unto you, it is easier for a camel to go through a needle's eye, than for a rich man to enter into the kingdom of God".

If the Universe has provided for your every need and desire and you have godlike abilities, why then would it be hard for a rich man to enter the kingdom? Despite the fact that those who have taught the dogmas are frequently surrounded by wealth, these lines are used to demonize the notion of wealth. These feelings are based in the fear that there is not enough to go around. If we set our minds, our kingdom, with the idea that only the few are deserving of wealth and riches, either materially or spiritually, that is the world we will create.

The "rich man" is one who seeks wealth or possessions as an end. The "rich man" knows it all and cares little for others. The "rich man" is trapped by the illusion and fears the loss of that illusion. Such a person has a very difficult time seeing and feeling the finer side of life. Such a person knows little of caring or sharing. Such a person is blind to the plenty that is freely given to all and, out of fear, cannot enter that space within where deeper and more lasting riches abide.

Based upon everything that Jesus has to say concerning the Law of Attraction and creating one's own reality, there can be little doubt that the Universe has no problem with each and every person sharing in its bounty. What it does say is that material bounty as an "end" will not fulfill your needs. As a means to an end, riches can be very useful and they can serve as a tool with which to bring happiness to many. A true "rich man" knows that the more that is given, the more that will be received. But a person of wealth who thinks that by giving he loses will face great difficulties finding the higher meaning of existence.

We are all "god like" in that we have the power to create, shape and mold reality. On a largely unconscious level we exercise this power every day. Our lack of understanding of our abilities enables others to dominate us and condition the world we seek to manifest. However, when we assume conscious control of this power, we find that others no longer control our thoughts. They no longer keep us in darkness. They no longer have the ability to press their erroneous views of life upon us.

"Go thy way; thy faith hath made thee whole."

Take whatever path you may desire, because your faith, your knowing has brought wholeness and truth into your life. This faith or knowing straightens the crooked road and smoothes out the bumps of life and brings a state of completeness or wholeness.

"Verily I say unto you, If ye have faith, and doubt not, ye shall not only do this which is done to the fig tree, but also if ye shall say unto this mountain, Be thou removed, and be thou cast into the sea; it shall be done. And all things, whatsoever ye shall ask in prayer, believing, ye shall receive."

The process outlined by Jesus is not for the dabbler. You cannot try it out to see if it works and then decide to accept or reject it later. If the roots are not deep, if the foundation of your thinking is built on sand, your mansion will crumble.

All things that you ask, KNOWING that it can be done, shall be done unto you. Reciting litanies or affirmations will not take you far on the manifestation highway. Further, if you KNOW that you will get cancer, if you KNOW that you will not get the job, if you KNOW you will not be able to pay your bills, if you KNOW that you will not get along with someone, if you KNOW that a nation is your enemy, then BELIEVING, you SHALL receive.

ALL things, whatsoever, you shall receive. Jesus did not say that you would only receive positive things. What is in the heart and comes out of your mouth determines your reality, for better or worse.

"Have faith in God. For verily I say unto you, That whosoever shall say unto this mountain, Be thou removed, and be thou cast into the sea; and shall not doubt in his heart, but shall believe that those things which he saith shall come to pass; he shall have whatsoever he saith."

If you believe that something will happen and have no doubts that it will happen, whatever you say WILL happen. The notion of faith in God is introduced. This does not imply that you must have faith in a particular god or religion, but only that you know that whatever God there is, it has deemed these laws to be the nature of the Universe. These laws work for Christians, Muslims, Hindus, Buddhist, Wic- cans, Shamans, anyone. They equally work for the agnostic or the atheist. No religion or belief can lay claim to the operating principles of nature.

"Therefore I say unto you, what things soever ye desire, when ye pray, believe that ye receive them, and ye shall receive them."

Whatever you desire is a lot different than whatever you need. No restrictions are placed upon your desires. When you pray, when you ask from the proper mindset and you believe that your desires are fulfilled, you shall receive them.

It is critical to understand that Jesus does not say that you will receive the things you desire. It is not in the future tense, it is in the present. Know that you receive and you shall receive.

If you have doubts, if your mind is cluttered with questions, if your desires are unclear or you are trying to test the principles, then you have knocked upon a door that will open to emptiness.

Desiring, asking, knowing, receiving, accepting, taking responsibility and expressing gratitude are key concepts that are inherent parts of the manifestation and attraction process.

"God is not the God of the dead, but of the living; for all live unto him: ye therefore do greatly err."

Your rewards do not come after death, in a mythical heaven. In the Universe, death is only a false appearance, an illusion, a trick of the eye. If you accept this as truth, then you will understand that all of the promises and riches promised by Jesus occur in the eternal now. This Now is ripe with harvest and awaits the eyes that see.

The Principles or Laws of Attraction, Responsibility, Manifestation and Gratitude have existed since the beginning of time.

There are those who have and still try to hoard these secrets and mysteries. Jesus said, **"For nothing is hidden that shall not become evident, nor anything secret that shall not be known and come to light."**

There are those who fear that the Universe has limits. There are those who have come to believe, and have thus created, the idea that some independent negative force may take the riches they have gained. Perhaps some had much and lost much. Not understanding the process, they decided that to regain their wealth they had to take rather than receive. As a result the Grand Illusion was manifested and the stage was set for the struggles that have plagued humanity for centuries. The losses and tragedies that have plagued human history can end on a positive turn of the Sacred Rota if we learn from past experiences. Combined with knowledge and understanding, these experiences lead to WISDOM.

Jesus knew that we would face a continuous struggle to reveal the hidden concepts in his messages. To alert us to these struggles Jesus left a lasting message to all who would search for the inner meaning of his words and parables. When he spoke of the scribes, Pharisees and hypocrites, he was not just referring to those in his time that would try to obstruct his ideas. He knew that he was timeless and that what he said then would be valid throughout the ages. In the context of all that has been revealed, read the following with a new understanding and apply the words to the present, not the past.

"But woe unto you, scribes and Pharisees, hypocrites! for ye shut up the kingdom of heaven against men: for ye neither go in yourselves, neither suffer ye them that are entering to go in.

Woe unto you, scribes and Pharisees, hypocrites! for ye pay tithe of mint and anise and cumin, and have omitted the weightier matters of the law, judgment, mercy, and faith: these ought ye to have done, and not to leave the other undone. Ye blind guides, which strain at a gnat, and swallow a camel.

Woe unto you, scribes and Pharisees, hypocrites! for ye make clean the outside of the cup and of the platter, but within they are full of extortion and excess. Thou blind Pharisee, cleanse first that which is within the cup and platter, that the outside of them may be clean also.

Woe unto you, scribes and Pharisees, hypocrites! for ye are like unto whited sepulchres, which indeed appear beautiful outward, but are within full of dead men's bones, and of all uncleanness. Even so ye also outwardly appear righteous unto men, but within ye are full of hypocrisy and iniquity.

Woe unto you, scribes and Pharisees, hypocrites! because ye build the tombs of the prophets, and garnish the sepulchres of the righteous, and say, If we had been in the days of our fathers, we would not have been partakers with them in the blood of the prophets.

Wherefore ye be witnesses unto yourselves, that ye are the children of them which killed the prophets. Fill ye up then the measure of your fathers. Ye serpents, ye generation of vipers, how can ye escape the damnation of hell?

Wherefore, behold, I send unto you prophets, and wise men, and scribes: and some of them ye shall kill and crucify; and some of them shall ye scourge in your synagogues, and persecute them from city to city: that upon you may come all the righteous blood shed upon the earth, from the blood of righteous Abel unto the blood of Zacharias son of Barachias, whom ye slew between the temple and the altar. Verily I say unto you, All these things shall come upon this generation.

O Jerusalem, Jerusalem, thou that killest the prophets, and stonest them which are sent unto thee, how often would I have gathered thy children together, even as a hen gathereth her chickens under her wings, and ye would not!

Behold, your house is left unto you desolate. For I say unto you, ye shall not see me henceforth, till ye shall say, Blessed is he that cometh in the name of the Lord.

Verily, verily, I say unto you, He that believeth on me, the works that I do shall he do also; and greater works than these shall he do; because I go unto my Father.

And whatsoever ye shall ask in my name, that will I do, that the Father may be glorified in the Son. If ye shall ask any thing in my name, I will do it.

If ye love me, keep my commandments. And I will pray the Father, and he shall give you another Comforter, that he may abide with you for ever; even the Spirit of truth; whom the world cannot receive, because it seeth him not, neither knoweth him: but ye know him; for he dwelleth with you, and shall be in you. I will not leave you comfortless: I will come to you.

Yet a little while, and the world seeth me no more; but ye see me: because I live, ye shall live also. At that day ye shall know that I am in my Father, and ye in me, and I in you.

Abide in me, and I in you. As the branch cannot bear fruit of itself, except it abide in the vine; no more can ye, except ye abide in me. I am the vine, ye are the branches: He that abideth in me, and I in him, the same bringeth forth much fruit: for without me ye can do nothing.

If a man abide not in me, he is cast forth as a branch, and is withered; and men gather them, and cast them into the fire, and they are burned. If ye abide in me, and my words abide in you, ye shall ask what ye will, and it shall be done unto you.

And in that day ye shall ask me nothing. Verily, verily, I say unto you, Whatsoever ye shall ask the Father in my name, he will give it you. Hitherto have ye asked nothing in my name: ask, and ye shall receive, that your joy may be full.

It is more blessed to give than to receive.

To him that overcometh will I give to eat of the tree of life, which is in the midst of the paradise of God.

I have highlighted some key phrases that require your further thought. Some will be quite obvious while others require your inner guidance. If you can get past the dogma built around some of these words you may see that not only do they add to the information in this work, they also dispel some of the myths surrounding these same words. Read the texts in the stream of thought contained in the previous chapters. Is the vine a person or is it a concept that speaks of deeper meaning? If we are connected to the vine are we not of the same family? What is the Comforter that is within each of us? Does Jesus put himself forward as someone to be worshipped or as someone to be emulated? Is there any separation between us and the Spirit of Truth or are we just blinded by the illusion?

Many have tried to suppress these messages and many have tried to deliver these messages. The ideas expressed by the Masters have been before our eyes for thousands of years but have been hid by our fears, blindness and lack of knowing. All spiritual leaders have told these truths in ways that make sense to the cultures in which they were delivered.

You are gods. You do control your own destiny and reality. You can have anything you desire. There are no limits to the supply of riches in the Universe. You are responsible for all of your actions. There is nothing outside of you that can cause you harm. What you are within, you express outwardly. What you believe, you attract. What you believe, you create. These words and phrases are being echoed like a spiritual shot heard around the world. The Great Awakening is upon us. Fear not, for there is no judgment, no punishment, and none will be left behind!

A CONCLUDING THOUGHT

I have covered the basic tenets of the **_Law of Attraction as taught by Jesus,_** but there are a few lines that need further emphasis.

For everyone that asketh receiveth; and he that seeketh findeth...

If a son shall ask bread of you that is a father, will he give him a stone? Or if he ask a fish, will he for a fish give him a serpent?

If ye then, being evil, know how to give good gifts unto your children: how much more shall your heavenly Father give the Holy Spirit to them that ask him?

It is so important that you understand some **_key words_** here. **_EVERYONE THAT ASKS WILL RECEIVE!_** There is no exclusion here. Rich, poor, wise, ignorant, fat, thin, tall skinny, white, black, sinner...EVERYONE that asks will receive.

Do you see any conditions in the words of Jesus? Does he say that if you go to church, put money in the plate or only live in America that you will receive? Did he exclude anyone by race, creed, color or national origin? EVERYONE SHALL RECEIVE!!!!!!.

Put an end to any notion that only a Christian is on the receive list. When Jesus lived, THERE WERE NO CHRISTIANS. You are entitled to receive no matter what your circumstance.

There are those who would have you believe that you can ask for what you want but you will only get what God decides you should get. That is simply not true. Ask for fish, you get fish, not a disease, not a stone, not a trial or tribulation—you get a fish. But others have convinced you that you may not deserve a fish so be thankful for what you get. Not true. God is not a "bait and switch" con artist. You get what you expect and what you believe and that is the Law of Attraction. If you ask for a fish, bread, good health, prosperity, loving relationships or a new job, you will not get a scorpion UNLESS you believe that you are unworthy to get what you ask for. You receive based upon the vibration of your true belief.

If being evil, which is really being ignorant, you give good things to your children, why would you possibly expect the UNIVERSE, GOD, the FATHER, to do less than you? There is no reason to believe that the Universe will make you run the gamut of trials and tribulations in order to receive what you truly desire.

There is a major key here… how much more shall your heavenly Father give the Holy Spirit to them that ask him? To what does the Universe, Father, give*? It gives to the HOLY SPIRIT of anyone that asks. Unto your HIGHER SELF, your HOLY SPIRIT, is given the keys to the Universe.* When you tap into your higher consciousness, all that you ask for and seek you will find and manifest. If you do not do this consciously, your are permitting the consciousness of others dictate your reality. You are letting others manifest your world.

You are given the power to seek, receive and to manifest fish, bread, and a happy and prosperous life.

THAT IS THE PROMISE!

TOOLS TO USE: JESUS AND THE LAW OF ATTRACTION

Jesus laid a set of principles regarding the manifestation of one's reality and desires. It is important to repeat that the cornerstone that he placed has nothing to do with one's religious belief or faith. There was no such thing as Christianity during his lifetime and his message was meant for all.

Based upon his stream of thought, it is possible to outline a specific pattern to follow, a specific mindset that is needed in order to work hand-in-hand with the Universe in the act of creation. The following outlines the essence of the teachings of Jesus on this topic. Use it as a checklist or a quick mental check to ensure your success in using The Law of Attraction.

1. **Your focus must be clear and not filled with excess "merchandise" or concern for day-to-day problems.**

2. **Realize that all of your needs and desires have already been met—the fields are ripe for harvest NOW.**

3. **Your mindset must be free and clear of judgments concerning your world. A judgment is a final decision and whatever you are convinced of in your mind will manifest in your world.**

4. **Change your mind about the nature of the world and know that the kingdom of heaven is here now, in each of you.**

5. **Let the inner light of your true nature be made manifest**

in your world.

6. You can be as perfect as the Universe. In fact, you are as perfect as the Universe. You just need to know it.

7. Take no concern for the basic necessities of life, they have been provided. See the abundance that is freely given to all. The Universe knows of your needs and has provided accordingly.

8. In order to attract that which you desire, you must find that part of you, the kingdom within, that has no doubts, that knows that all of your desires are fulfilled are now.

9. Everything in your life is a result of your thoughts and intentions. This is The Law of Responsibility. Denial of this fact may close doors that lead to the kingdom within.

10. You cannot expect to manifest your desires if your mind set is one that believes in lack and scarcity in the Universe. If you are not convinced within, you will not alter what you perceive to be without. You cannot put new wine in old bottles.

11. If your thoughts are divided and you lack confidence and surety, your mental house will collapse.

12. Thinking you know it all does not work if you have only information but little inner conviction.

13. Whatever you decide the world is, that is how it will be.

14. If you want to know how you really think and feel, merely examine your life. The fruits that you see are your own thoughts made manifest.

15. Whatever you believe, that is the way your life and world will be.

16. Once you establish an inner conviction that the laws work, you become a magnet of positive energy. To him that has, more is give. This is The Law of Attraction.

17. There is nothing within that does not appear without.

18. Beware of the beliefs and ideas that you allow to enter your mind.

19. Eliminate all fears, they attract what you least desire.

20. The field of harvest is in our minds. When you try to alter your entire belief system do not be surprised if your negative thoughts try to strike back and re-take control of your life. Old ways die-hard.

21. Contrary to appearance and belief, there is literally nothing outside of you that can harm you.

22. It is only what you express from the depths of your thoughts, emotions, and intentions and words that can have a negative impact on your life.

23. There is a difference between information and "knowing."

24. Nothing is impossible.

25. You are gods and if you ask, seek, and knock, you will receive. The door will be opened.

26. What you have received, what you have found and the doors that have been opened are of your own doing.

27. If you seek the truth of your inner being, all that you need and desire will be manifest in your life.

28. Always be ready to hear the inner voice of inspiration and guidance.

29. Whatever you desire, know that you have it and you will have it.

30. Your rewards are for the now, not the afterlife.

31. There is no separation between you, God, Jesus and the entire Universe.

32. Ask, know (believe), receive, give thanks and share.

33. The path to the kingdom is through the inner self and not through any person, including Jesus. He is the WAY means that the inner self is the door. You can only change yourself, not others.

THE POWER OF GRATITUDE

In a polite society we say "thank you" after we receive a gift. While that is nice, it not exactly the way the Universe works. Many falter in the manifestation process because they believe that they do not already have what they want. After all, if you cannot see it or touch it, it is not there right? Wrong! Anything and everything that you could possibly want or desire is all around you. It is in the form of energy waiting to be shaped and brought into the physical world by the creative process of the mind.

Thoughts are things and all things are made of energy—Physics 101. Nothing exists in the world that was not first thought about. A chair, a house, a plane, a computer, etc. are merely thoughts that have become manifest. I would go so far as to say that you and all the infinite manifestations of life exist because of the first thought— the prime mover—the creative consciousness behind all of existence.

When we say that we do not have something, we close the cosmic door. We are telling the Universe "I do not have" and the Universe grants your desire and thus you do not have. It is said, "seek, and you shall find, knock and the door shall be opened." Unfortunately most people think this merely means that if you seek spiritual salvation, you will find it. However, these words are a basic Law of the Universe. In essence the law says that if you seek something, you will find it. It also says that what you have found is what you have sought. If you knock, a door will be opened, or the doors that have opened are the ones upon which you have knocked.

This puts life squarely upon your shoulders. What you have gotten is what you have sought. "But," you say, "I did not seek disease, poverty, financial lack, poverty, loneliness or general misery." You either consciously did or you unconsciously accepted these conditions because someone convinced you that is all you will ever get out of life. Someone gives you a canvas and some paints and you say, "What good is this? There is no picture on the canvas. It is blank." You are told to draw a picture and you balk because you are convinced that you are not an artist. As a result, other people use the paints to draw what they want. Now you are stuck with a picture that someone else painted and that you do not like.

Now you sit, displeased with the picture but unwilling to change it because you are convinced that only others can paint. What does this have to do with gratitude? Because you do not feel that you can paint, you do not feel any level of thankfulness for the pictures others have drawn for you. You really wanted a picture of a beautiful house in the country but someone draws a rundown apartment. Why should you be thankful, the picture is not what you want?

The fact of the matter is that you do have whatever you want. The canvas is all things. It merely awaits your brush strokes to make it real. When you say that you have nothing to be thankful for, you are saying that the canvas can never have the picture you desire. You close the door without even trying to open it. You see the canvas as blank, but it can be whatever you desire it to be.

Giving thanks means that you have already received something. When you give thanks to the Universe for all that you could possibly desire, you are saying that you have received all that you could possibly desire. You give form and then substance to the energy that exists everywhere and by law, these things must manifest. If you say that the picture on the canvas is a new house, it cannot be a rundown apartment. The painting can only be what is put on it.

It is only hard to give thanks for what you think you do not have because that is your conditioning. You can't paint? Not true! The world you have, you have painted. When you begin to accept the fact that you are the artist of your own life, you will begin to realize that all of those blank canvasses await your secret desires to be drawn by your creative mind.

Give thanks for all that you desire. They already exist in potential. It is up to you to make them real. Tell the Universe what you want and tell the Universe you are thankful that it has given you an unlimited supply of paint. Do not close the door of life by saying, no, thank you.

THE FINE ART OF VISUALIZATION I

The Universe operates according to set laws and the co-creators need to be aware of those laws if they are to be successful in their efforts to consciously create their own reality. Keep yourself in mind. You are constantly creating your reality, albeit on an unconscious level. If you want to know what you think about the most, what you are emotional about and what you believe in strongly, all you need to do is look at your life. Your current reality is merely a reflection of what is occurring in your mind.

Visualization is a key to creating your own reality. If you think that you cannot visualize, you are mistaken, since the world you see is the result of your visualization. The Universe is very literal. It does not judge your desires. It will create what you hold in your mind, thoughts and emotions.

It should be stated clearly from the outset you cannot create negative thoughts or send negative thoughts to someone. All that happens in that situation is that you pollute your own mind and affect only yourself and your perception of the world. There is more that could be said here, but it is not worth the energy to do so.

Visualization is more than just seeing what you want in your mind. It is not a flat image like on a TV screen but rather contains all the dimensions and the physical and emotional senses. In a way, it is a hologram in which you must be an active participant if you are to achieve maximum success. Most people start off on the wrong foot when it comes to visualization. They start with the premise "I want." Like I said, the Universe is very literal and so it will give you all the "wanting" you can handle. Any verb that follows "I" is very powerful and it is the key message to the Universe. Therefore, if you say, "I want more money," this is interpreted by the Universe as you "want" to keep wanting more money. What you get is merely "wanting" and basically no money. This holds true for phrases like "I need," "I wish," "I hope," etc. If you think like this, all you will manifest is "needing, wishing and hoping" in abundance.

Here is a key; there is nothing that you do not have. Since all things are made of energy, and there is an unlimited supply of energy in the Universe, truly there is no shortage. All that you could ever want or desire exists and is merely waiting for you to bring it into your life. When you tell the Universe "I have financial abundance, perfect health, a great personal relationship, spiritual enlightenment, and a wonderful and joyous life," then you set the Universe in motion and it ensures that what you "have" in your mind is brought into physical reality. It is not that seeing is believing; it is rather believing is seeing. Better yet, knowing is receiving.

Knowing that you have what you desire sets up a receptive mental state. Now is the time to act "as if." In your mind, you add dimension and emotion to that which you have mentally created. If it is a home improvement you desire, in your mind, you see yourself in the added room along with all of the decorations, furnishings, smells and activities you will do there. See other family members in the room and play out in your mind conversations and other things you will do in that added space. Make it real. Pick the colors of the walls and see yourself hanging the paintings and then just feel good that what you created mentally is now real.

Do not be concerned how this becomes reality and always keep the vision in the present tense. I have, not I will have. The word "will" implies future and, as I said, the Universe is literal; that future will always remain in the future until you accept your vision in the now.

Do not second-guess how your vision will occur. Many fail at this stage. They try to prescribe to the Universe how it should materialize the vision. I knew a person who once tried to manifest the "money" for her perfect new car. She kept failing. She was telling the Universe that the only way she could get the new car was to get money. After some consultation she decided not to tell the Universe but rather to let the Universe do its own thing. She began to visualize the car and her in it, period. A very short time later she was left the exact car, down to the red color by a relative who could no longer drive. The relative was going to sell the car but decided to give it to her niece instead, at no cost!

When you try to prescribe the means you actually close doors and oftentimes block the Universe from manifesting your vision. Do not get caught in the mental trap of "I want it and this is how it must come." The Universe is very resourceful.

There is another key step in this process and I would refer you to my other article, "The Power of Gratitude" posted on Gather. Now that you "have," be grateful. Let the Universe know that you appreciate the gift and are thankful for a Universe that is waiting and ready to meet all of your desires. Keep in mind that the Universe is not seeking gratitude, it really seeks nothing. But when you set up in your mind the attitude of gratitude, you make the manifestation of your vision real to you and that is what is important. One rarely gives thanks for something they have not received.

If you want, decorate your fridge with pictures and post sayings of gratitude—reminders of what you have already received. Every little bit helps.

THE FINE ART OF VISUALIZATION II

We live and breathe and have our existence in a sea of energy that is shaped, molded and manifest through conscious thought. All that exists is thought made manifest. To the ancient mystics, this was called the tapestry of life. In modern times, it is the string theory of quantum physics. Remember, there is no lack of energy in the Universe.

DO NOT give any attention to things that you do not want in your life. All that does is to feed energy into that which you do not desire. Do not adopt the attitude that there is no way that you can have what you desire simply because you do not see how it can come about. If the Universe can create stars, planets and life it is quite capable of creating a more positive situation for your life.

Even if you think you only have a little of what life seems to offer, it is necessary to be thankful for what you do have. This begins to put into motion the idea that what you have, you enjoy and the Universe will respond with more of what makes you happy. If you seem to have a lack of funds, be thankful for what you do have and let the Universe know that it pleases you to have money in the bank. This opens the door to more.

NEVER bemoan the fact that you cannot pay a bill, because if you do, then that is where you are putting your mental energy and the Universe responds by adding to that energy.

The Universe merely follows your flow of mental energy and adds to it. It makes no judgment about what you think about, it merely follows the flow of your thoughts and assumes that because you are filling that thought with your emotional energy, then it must be something you desire.

Once you have formed the picture of what you have (remember, you have everything, you just want to manifest it), do NOT dwell on the image to the point of distraction. If you keep changing your ideas then the Universe is given the impression that you have not finished your mental creation and so it will wait until you are done.

However, there is more that you can do to reinforce your mental creation. For the sake of argument, say you are seeking a new or more positive relationship. You have imagined (imaged) your perfect partner. What you can now do is a little daydreaming. Picture what you and your new partner will be doing. See yourself and your partner going out to dinner, attending a play or concert, taking a drive or spending a quiet moment together. What are you going to talk about with your new mate? How will you spend your evenings? What clothes is he or she wearing?

In this daydream you do not alter the image; rather, you give it life and solidity. Fill it with conversation, laughter, emotion and a sense of joy and gratitude that all that you sought is real and now in your life. Do not make this a future event; see it in the now, for now is all that there is.

This bringing to life of your image is often overlooked. If a car is your desire, then see yourself in it and going places. If it is better health, then see yourself doing what you desire in a state of wholeness. If it is enlightenment you seek, feel the presence of revelation, higher knowledge and understanding flowing through every fiber of your being. Want to help world peace? Then do not see the world at war but rather focus upon a vision of the world filled with understanding and brotherly love.

As you focus upon these energies, they are drawn into your world by the Law of Attraction. Remember, you cannot change the lives of others and impose your will upon others. We are each responsible for our own reality. By drawing in the energies you desire, you do have an effect upon others. Remember, the Universe is a tapestry and all of the threads are connected. As you re-create your part of the picture, the entire mosaic begins to take on a new and more positive appearance. Align yourself with positive thoughts and the world will follow your example.

Breathe life into your images and fill them with emotion, passion and life. See, feel, taste and hear your creation into existence. One last word of caution; do not fantasize. While there are no limits except what we limit in our minds, there are laws that you cannot alter, at least on this plane and in this place. You will not be able to sprout wings and fly, at least not physically. If you have no singing voice at all but want to be a big rock star, then be prepared to take music lessons. If you do not know how to turn on a computer, you will not wake up a Webmaster the next morning. The Universe may provide you with the means and opportunities to manifest some of these desires, but until you achieve a higher level of spiritual mastership it is probably best to keep your desires in the realm of possibility. While all things are possible, not all things are probable.

AN INTERVIEW WITH DR. JOHN DEMARTINI

Dr. John Demartini, THE SECRET,
and Transforming the World:
A One-on-One Interview
Part I

On November 2nd Dr John Demartini appeared as a panel guest on The Larry King Show called "Beyond Positive Thinking." In a highly simplified explanation, the panel discussed how people could truly alter their reality through techniques presented in the film phenomena The Secret. Saying that these techniques are based upon true science and not fantasy, the panelists discussed the notion that each person has the scientifically proven ability to alter their physical, mental and emotional reality in order to manifest their own desires. From curing diseases, finding soul-mates, finding the perfect job, to attaining wealth, no aspect of one's life is beyond the capacity of the mind. The show was a success. A second show was presented on November 16th and subsequent shows on the same topic have been planned.

After the show I wrote an article for The American Chronicle and several blogs which asked the question, "If this information was accurate, why do people live such miserable lives?" As a lifelong student of mysticism, I firmly believe in the principles discussed on the show and presented in the film and, for that matter, presented in my co-authored book, WAKING GOD. However, I felt that a key topic was missing in the discussion and my article went on to present my own theories as to the greatest impediment that confronts humanity in utilizing these principles (See 11/6 article www.americanchronicle.com). The article was read by Dr.

Demartini and his publicist, Cloud Nine Marketing, and I received an email from Cloud Nine asking if I wanted to do an interview with John. Who could refuse? On November 22nd I talked with John for about an hour. He was at a Las Vegas hotel and was preparing for a seminar he was going to give that evening.

I did not want to ask John questions that would be a repeat of those on the Larry King Show, nor did I want to delve deeply into his early childhood or reiterate a biography that can be readily found on his web site www.drdemartini.com. For those who have yet to experience his magic, I will simply say that John is a millionaire, an international speaker, author and business consultant. He heads the Demartini Foundation and the Concourse of Wisdom School. According to his web site he was told at the age of six that he had a learning disability and would never read, write or communicate. John obviously walks his talk and creates his own reality.

I was looking to focus on the issues I raised in my article about the show. What has kept The Secret from being utilized by all? The principles upon which it is based can be traced to the ancient mystery schools of the Egyptian and Mayan civilizations. Why have only the few had access to this wisdom? Why is it coming to light now? What are the obstacles that seem to prevent all from creating a new life of happiness and harmony? My first question to John was whether or not there was a single moment in which he decided that the "normal" way of doing things was not right for him? Was there any particular person or book that altered his way of thinking and sent him on a new path of thought?

John indicated that there was no single event or book that he would classify as the impetus for his personal transformation. Instead, over twenty years of studying philosophy and cosmology led him to discover a set of common concepts, ideas, laws and patterns that were universally accepted 'truths.' He said, "I devoured 'ologies' and any book that dealt with positive thinking."

At the age of 18, he read the works of Gandhi and decided to embark upon a self-monitored effort to change his own thought behavior. Four times a day he checked to see if his thoughts were more positive and he made every effort to make them positive. After two years he came to the startling conclusion that he did in fact create his own paradigm shift. Over the two-year period he discovered that his thoughts balanced between positive and negative thinking. Despite his efforts to always stay positive, over time there was always a balance.

His conclusion was that the laws of the universe would always be fulfilled and that, indeed, there is always a plus for every minus, every action creates an opposite reaction. He indicated that by embracing both we are working in concert with the universe—the key being how to find the benefits accrued from both sides of the coin.

As a personal clarification, let me equate this to the idea of waking and sleeping. You may want to be on the 'go' all day and accomplish much, the plus side of life. You may then view sleep as negative since it interferes with your desire to do other things. We all know that it is during sleep that body regenerates itself and so what appears negative on the surface is actually beneficial. The same could be said for illness; that is the body's way of telling you that some aspect of your being is not in balance and needs correction.

The dis-ease, as they said on the show, may appear negative but actually can become positive if one makes the effort to correct the imbalance and to prevent it from occurring again. John said that in every aspect of nature and in life there is the build up phase and the destroy phase and yet these phases also occur simultaneously. He said somewhere on earth it is winter, somewhere it is summer. Cities are being built and others are in decay. Life is a balance and the key is to discover how both sides of this building and destruction can be of benefit.

I asked John what he felt were the greatest impediments for people as they tried to use the principles in The Secret. In other words, for the average guy on the street what is going to prevent them from creating their own reality? John said that there are seven primary fears that immobilize people and the first one is the fear of breaking the moral and ethics of some spiritual authority. That is, subordination to perceived spiritual authorities and the fear of breaking the rights and wrongs of that authority stops people.

The second one is the fear of not being smart enough, not having a degree, not having the intelligence and not being imaginative enough.

The third one is the fear that you're going to fail at it. I don't want to start because I know I'm going to be a failure.

The forth one is the idea that I won't make money at it, it costs too much money or I'll lose money doing it.

The fifth one is the fear of losing a loved one's respect

The next one is the fear of somehow being rejected by the general audience, people in society. Are you crazy, why are you doing, this is stupid and ridiculous.

Last thing is the fear of ill health, death or disease. You don't have the body to do it, the looks for it, the height or strength necessary.

Those seven fears make people lie to themselves about what they really want. They immobilize themselves.

John went on to say that people set up fantasies that are not what they truly want and that are not aligned with the laws of the Universe. These fantasies will not manifest and then people get discouraged and go around discouraging others. And so the endless cycle of unrealistic desires dashed lead to the notion that people do not have control of their lives.

The issues was raised as to whether or not a person can just sit in a room and manifest their true desires without having to take any action. John indicated that "you have to work your butt off—you'll have no ass when you are done." He said that you cannot merely imagine what you without taking any action to bring those desires into reality.

When people ask him how he got where he is today, he reiterates that he had to work his butt off. The people that persevere are the ones that get results. He added that there is no doubt that when the mind is clear and precise and inspired this assists in the process but to visualize is a small piece of the puzzle unless accompanied by action.

DR. JOHN DEMARTINI: THE SECRET AND TOILER PAPER: A ONE-ON-ONE INTERVIEW

Part II

I asked John if there was any particular reason why the film "The Secret" was released at this time. In other words, is there anything about the present situation in the world that makes the publicizing of these once hidden techniques more appropriate now, than say ten years ago?

He indicated that perhaps the people were in the right place at this time to bring the information to light. Rhonda Byrne had developed a deep appreciation for the laws of the universe and, with her production company in Australia, she had the will and the means to share ways to help people. It "just so happened" that many of the people that appeared in the film were attending a leadership and transformational meeting in Aspen, and Rhonda brought her TV crew to the meeting and was able to tape major portions of the film at that location. This combined with the modern age of technology and the vast networks represented by the film's participants enabled the film and its message to reach millions upon millions of people that might otherwise have been left wanting.

Is there a "secret agenda?" Being a Rosicrucian I could not help but notice the frequency with which the word Rosicrucian flashed between speakers in the film. John indicated that "wisdom is wisdom" and anyone who searches out universal laws will run into the various lists of secret organizations. He thought that some of the people connected to the movie were probably Rosicrucian and that he also, in addition to studying Mayan and other mystery teachings, had also studied Rosicrucian teachings. This relatively sequestered order has come to the forefront of late and is receiving greater publicity. However, John felt that there is only a sincere altruistic desire on the part of those connected to the film to bring much that has been hidden into the mainstream for all to share.

Trying to glance ahead, I asked John where he saw the world in 2012 and if he felt that there was enough time, given the current state of world affairs and changing climatic conditions, to turn things around for humanity before possible global disaster. John's response should be a lesson and inspiration for all because I do not believe that there is a negative bone left in his body. John said, "I do not see anything in the world that is going to stop human development. I am certainly not frightened by anything that is going on. I see that there are always two sides to an event. If we look for one side, the down side, we go into doomsday; if we look at the up side we go into fantasyland. But if we look at both of them we see that nature is simply remodeling things and whoever has the clearest intention is the one that moves it in that direction ... I truly believe that there is a field of intelligence that is far greater than our human intellect and I think that it is doing fine and that we are just waking up to it and we're learning along the way and we remodel ourselves accordingly. But I really don't have any fear about what's going on in the world. I see a balance. I see that there is build and destroy. If you look at the earth from the most ancient times you see that there was spring and fall, somewhere on the world at all times. Summer and winter is always somewhere, so what you have is build and destroy ... And so humans are manifesting the course of build and destroy and remodeling in their cities, their own physiology, in our thoughts we build ourselves up and beat ourselves down. In nature we do it. In our cities we do it. In our environment we do it."

Probing this a little further, I asked if John felt that society had hit rock bottom and that there was a lot of fear in the world. John said that he did not wake each morning with fear for what is happening in the world. He said, "I look at things in such a way where I ask how does whatever happened to me, either positive or negative, serve me." He went on to say that, "Fear is an assumption that you are about to experience more pain than pleasure, more loss than gain, more negative than positive, more challenge than support, from somebody or yourself. If we have those perceptions, then of course we are going to react and withdraw. Fear is really an unrealistic expectation. It is wiser to go back and look at the balance of things so the fear dissolves. As Buckminster Fuller said, pollution is simply a resource we have yet to find a use for."

John added that we need to find the order hidden in our daily chaos and that despite polarity; he feels that the world has a heart.

We then explored the notion of "divine intelligence." John said, "To those who believe, no proof is necessary; to those who don't, no proof is possible; and it is not wise to waste words on those who seek not."

He then mentioned the Demartini Method, a very profound way of helping people see that the events that are occurring in their life are synchronous, are synthesized and imply an intelligence far greater than our awareness. He said that he can demonstrate this repeatedly on very deep levels and in such a profound way that it literally involves the physics of life. He sees these concepts growing in strength and in numbers and infiltrating the business, financial, educational and scientific communities.

I could not help but wonder if John felt that he still had any barriers that he personally had left to cross. Was there anything in his life that he would like to alter? The response is a lesson for all, since we often go through life beating ourselves up for things we think we should or could have done differently.

John said, "I don't think of it that way. No matter what I've done or not done, I'm worthy of love. Any time I think I need some kind of fixing it's because I haven't looked at myself more thoroughly. So I don't put myself into a moral illusion that I need improvement or any of those things. Albert Einstein said something: 'If God is omnipotent and omnipresent and omniscient then every human action, reaction and aspiration in life is part of the Divine Plan'. So I don't look back and say, oops, I messed up here, I should have done this or should have done that. I don't live that way."

With regard to what changes he would like to see on a worldwide scale he said, "That there would be toilet paper in all the johns across the world." On a serious vein, he said that he felt that all the people on the entire planet have within them a deep sense of love, they just do not see it.

He indicated that it is not about fixing the world because when you focus on fixing you create the equal and opposite and thereby actually add to the problems. People need to see the magnificence of themselves and the world in which they live and love people and the world for whom and what it is; this is what creates the transformation.

Bringing up my co-authored book, WAKING GOD, I mentioned that we felt (myself and co-author Brian Doe) that religion was perhaps the single most important obstacle people had to overcome in order to utilize the principles of The Secret. The interview was winding down but we began to discuss this issue in a way that may upset those "who seek not." John said, "When we subordinate ourselves to the religious systems, we basically stop opening up our religious heart."

Can you practice The Secret and do 'Hail Marys' at the same time was my next line of thought. John replied, "That is contradictory. I would say that if there is a divine order, divine intelligence and divine love and divine wisdom and beauty in everything, then where is God not?" He explained that if we think we see some place or person where we think God is not then we must re-examine ourselves and our own perceptions about what we think we see. If we see something out of order, then it is our job to go back and to look again.

John indicated that any human being we see on the outside reflects what is on our inside. If there is something that you cannot love about them then there is a part of you that you feel is unworthy of love. Because the universe is from a single source, all is connected and all is entangled.

This raised the last question concerning the role that our subconscious mind plays in impeding our personal growth. John said that we develop values based upon what we think we are missing or lacking in life. If we lack money, we value money; if we lack love, we value love; if we lack a nice home, friends or a good job, we place them in our value system. Whatever is most perceived as missing, we value. We view and act upon the world according to these values. Then we see those that appear to have all that we perceive we lack, a.k.a. movie stars, business leaders, etc. We now subordinate ourselves to them. We feel that they have what we lack. By putting these people on a pedestal, we subordinate ourselves to them and their values. Now our own true values recede into our subconscious. We are now trying to be someone else, someone we are not. We attempt to imitate these other people. Now our world is filled with shoulds and ought to haves. But we still have our own values that become subconscious and another's values become conscious and we act like somebody we are not. This raises a moral dilemma. We now try to do something that is not ours. Perhaps we try to be a singer, artist or writer, and yet we really have no talent for these occupations. We aspire to be an actor but we have no acting ability. Now you bang your head against the wall trying to be someone you are not. You have entered a fantasy world and efforts to manifest that reality are bound to fail. Our desires must be true and congruent if we are to create our reality utilizing the principles in The Secret.

I asked John if he felt there was a kind of conspiracy to prevent the masses from utilizing the principles of The Secret. Ever the politician, John answered that if you challenge another's existing paradigm and value systems, they will close it off and try to prevent it. All is linked and we must learn to love everyone, no matter whom or what they are.

I told John that he should consider being a foreign policy advisor. He said that several years back he did send a letter to President Bush and to Donald Rumsfeld. The problem was that when he addressed the letter, he sent it to Ronald Dumsfeld. He said that it was not intentional. He did receive a letter back from the President saying "we have everything under control."

JESUS AND THE LAW OF ATTRACTION (ARTICLE)

There are 10.4 million sites on the internet devoted to the Law of Attraction and 168 million sites devoted to the topic of Jesus. Is there any relationship between these two phenomena? In the book and movie, "The Secret" it is claimed that the Law of Attraction has been kept secret for millennia. Is this true?

The answer to that question is a definitive yes, and no. The Law of Attraction, if you follow the claims of "secret societies," goes back to ancient Egypt. It takes some careful analysis but the claims are essentially correct, in my opinion. However, what is more certain is that this concept has been in plain sight for over 2,000 years. Like the proverbial purloined letter, the Law of Attraction has been in millions of homes around the world in the teachings of Jesus.

All too often, the sayings of Jesus are taken out of context. It is rare to actually see what he had to say in the complete context of his teachings. If you examine his whole "stream of thought" on a topic, what results is a meaning and idea that frequently goes against what is taught as religious dogma. This is the case with the Law of Attraction. Given that many Christian "hard liners" spoke out against the concepts presented in "The Secret" and the Law of Attraction, I decided to take a closer examination of the actual sayings attributed to Jesus as they may relate to this subject. What I found, and have documented in my recently released book, "Jesus Taught It, Too: The Early Roots of the Law of Attraction," was that Jesus was a strong advocate of this principle. He further talked about what has commonly been termed the "create your own reality" ideology and he actually introduced what I have termed, The Law of Responsibility.

Many have argued that these so called "laws" are not at all scientific and have no basis in the physical sciences. Equal arguments have been put forth by some scientists that they are, in fact, physical laws. That is a debate best left for others but recent advances in quantum physics at least suggests that there is more than meets the eye when it comes to how energy forces in the universe are organized and manipulated. To avoid that debate, let us just say that these are "spiritual laws." I would have to say that few could argue with the basic premise, not including magnetism or electricity that like minded people tend to aggregate together. People join in groups, unions or marriages because they share similar interests. Animals form herds for mutual benefit, "birds of a feather flock together," and even microscopic creatures form colonies. Is this a physical law? Perhaps it is but at a minimum the concept cannot be ignored in dealing with the notion that "like attracts like." From political parties, book clubs, ethnic clubs, sports teams and other social groupings, the operating principle is that similar ideas are attracted to one another.

After all, does not religion spread because people come to share a common theology? It seems that whenever someone in the pulpit teaches the words of Jesus, it is always in the context of serving the church, not sinning, being faithful to god, worship and other concepts that perpetuate the need for the pulpit. What is not usually taught or examined is that Jesus taught about how to live your everyday life. He knew people were concerned about putting food on the table and a roof over their head. He saw that people were ill, poor and lacking in personal freedom. It is in this context that he put forward sets of principles and formulas that would enable people to live a happy life and not one of poverty stricken servitude and mindless worship. Jesus taught that the "fields were already white with harvest" and that the "guiding intelligence" of the universe saw to it that all needs and desires are met. These promises, contrary to what some would have you believe, were unconditional and required no servitude or worship. They only required an open mind that could pierce through the cloak of ignorance and blind obedience in order to see the light of truth.

THE MANIFESTATION CATCH-22

If we can manifest our own reality, why is it that you seem to have a problem getting started? Aside from the largest issue being that you think that someone else, a "higher authority" has told you that it cannot be done and that it is a foolish notion, why can't you just give it a try. Of course, that is Catch-22 number one. You only want a test drive and you are fully aware that there are many things to try.

But, for the sake of argument, let's say that you are going to be sincere in your effort. You have heard a lot about the Law of Attraction and you actually believe that it can be done and are convinced that others have been successful. You decide that the most pressing issue, at the moment, in your life is the lack of financial resources so that will be your first goal, to manifest some money. Catch-22! The catch is that you tell the Universe you lack financial resources so "lack" is your message.

You put all of your bills into a stack and figure out how much money you need. Catch-22! You are telling the Universe that you are needy. You then come up with a firm amount-could be a Catch-22-you are saying that is all you need. You then tell the Universe that you want to win the lottery to pay off you bills. Catch-22! Maybe the Universe has a better way to pay the bills that does not include the lottery. You buy some tickets and get angry that you do not win. Catch-22! Your anger gives power to you idea of financial deficiency.

Time for a different approach?   You look at you bank statement and get concerned that you do not have enough money. Obvious Catch-22! You then decide that you are going to visualize your bank account with a certain sum. That's okay in a way but you have in the back of your mind that your account needs more money. Catch-22! You sit back waiting for your checking account to grow. Catch-22! You are not taking any action. When it doesn't, you get depressed, Catch-22, and you decide that the Law of Attraction is a bunch of bull. The Big Catch-22!

For those of you who are not familiar with Catch-22 it the title of a book by Joseph Heller. The notion is something like this. If you want to move to the U.S. you have to have a job. To have a job in the U.S. you must live here. That is the concept of Catch-22.

I offer the following from Dan Stone on The Shower Channel, "It can be a very difficult thing for you to hear and accept that you never really improve any situation by focusing on what's going wrong. You never really solve a problem by focusing on the problem. You never get yourself to a place that feels better by focusing on what feels bad (but don't tell the psychologists that).

A more precise and important way of putting it is that you cannot move forward in the direction of your dreams and desires when you are focused on the fear or the worry of failure. You cannot move in the direction of what you want when you are insisting upon staring at what is, where you are.

In fact we would encourage you to never pay attention to what is unless it is delightful to do so. Never give your attention to "what's real" or "what's true" unless that reality or that truth feels joyful or hopeful or comforting or reassuring or encouraging . ... For as long as you are giving your attention to anything that distresses or concerns or confuses or frustrates or scares you . . . then you are holding yourself in a place where the joy or the fulfillment or the love or the appreciation or the satisfaction cannot flow freely to you. You are stuck in a place that feels bad and you are stuck there for no reason other than that being what you are choosing to focus on."

I hope that you can see the Catch-22 in all of this. The moment you try to solve a problem you are sending out mixed messages. You are affirming you have the problem. You are focusing attention on the problem and giving it energy. You are keeping it alive because where your thoughts and emotions go, so does the Law of Attraction. We are told to "take no thought...the fields are already white with harvest and if you have, more will be given." The point is that when you give energy to a problem, you get more of the problem. What you give thought to is what the Universe will focus on. If you say you do not have, then you do not see the harvest in your life. If you focus on getting, the Universe responds by giving you getting. But, if you focus upon having, the Universe gives you more of what you have. Where your emotions go, the Universe goes also.

These are just some of the Catch-22's. You must be ever vigilant about your thoughts and emotions. If your desire is money, tell the Universe you really like money and that you are thankful for the money in your life. Do not look down upon the lowly penny but rather give thanks for every penny you have or find. Gives thanks for every bill that you pay and be joyous that you are able to spread the wealth and share with others, even if they are the bill collectors.

Focus upon the "have" and not the have not. Remember, every word that follows "I" is very powerful and sends a message to the Universe. Avoid using I want, I need, I don't, I should, I wish, I need, etc.

I do not mean to focus upon money but it is such an easy example to use. The same applies to every aspect of life and all of your emotions. Do not hold yourself in place by focusing upon your current situation. Walk, talk, think and plan with an attitude of already having. When you change your mindset, things will begin to change and the Catch-22s will begin to fade from your life.

QUOTES TO PONDER

There are literary thousands of quotes from thousands of spiritual, religious and mystical leaders. The few that are offered here are to highlight the fact that Jesus was not alone in his thinking with respect to such ideas as attraction, responsibility and manifestation. The underlying theme of all great spiritual thought is the unity of life, its eternal continuity and its divine right to forge its own reality in order to experience the illusion we call reality. The meaning of these quotes is a matter of personal interpretation but with inner thought you will see that all is not as it appears and that humanity has a destiny that far surpasses the dogma that has been taught throughout the ages.

Bodhidharma (c. 440 AD - 528 AD)
Source: The Zen Teaching of Bodhidharma

The essence of the Way is detachment. And the goal of those who practice is freedom from appearances.

When we're deluded, there's a world to escape. When we're aware, there's nothing to escape.

If you use your mind to study reality, you won't understand either your mind or reality. If you study reality without using your mind, you'll understand both. . . . The mind and the world are opposites, and vision arises where they meet. When your mind doesn't stir inside, the world doesn't arise outside. When the world and the mind are both transparent, this is true vision. And such understanding is true understanding.

Everything good and bad comes from your own mind. To find something beyond the mind is impossible.

If you know that everything comes from the mind, don't become attached. Once attached, you're unaware. But once you see your own nature, the entire Canon becomes so much prose. It's thousands of sutras and shastras only amount to a clear mind. Understanding comes in midsentence. What good are doctrines? The ultimate Truth is beyond words. Doctrines are words. They're not the Way. The Way is wordless. Words are illusions. . . . Don't cling to appearances, and you'll break through all barriers. . .

We do not see things as they are. We see them as we are.
The Talmud

There are two rules on the spiritual path: Begin and Continue.
Sufi saying

I believe in a Spinoza's God who reveals himself in the harmony of all that exists, but not in a God who concerns himself with the fate and actions of human beings.
Albert Einstein

Everyone who is seriously involved in the pursuit of science becomes convinced that a spirit is manifest in the laws of the.
Albert Einstein

In their struggle for the ethical good, teachers of religion must have the stature to give up the doctrine of a personal God, that is, give up that source of fear and hope which in the past placed such vast power in the hands of the priests."
Albert Einstein

The priests, in control of education, made the class division of society into a permanent institution and created a system of values by which the people were thenceforth, to a large extent unconsciously, guided in their social behavior.
Albert Einstein

It is not God who is hostile, but we; for God is never hostile.
St. John Chrysostom

The purposes of God point to one simple end—that we should be as he is, think the same thoughts, mean the same things, possess the same blessedness.
George MacDonald

There is only one reality. That reality is God. The soul of man must contact God, and unless the spirit of man is truly joined to God, there is no such thing as real Christian manifestation. John G. Lake
I searched for God and found only myself. I searched for myself and found only God.
Sufi Proverb

Buddhism does not accept a theory of God, or a creator. According to Buddhism, one's own actions are the creator, ultimately. Some people say that, from a certain angle, Buddhism is not a religion but rather a science of mind. Religion has much involvement with faith.

Sometimes it seems that there is quite a distance between a way of thinking based on faith and one entirely based on experiment, remaining skeptical. Unless you find something through investigation, you do not want to accept it as fact. From one viewpoint, Buddhism is a religion, from another viewpoint Buddhism is a science of mind and not a religion. Buddhism can be a bridge between these two sides. Therefore, with this conviction I try to have closer ties with scientists, mainly in the fields of cosmology, psychology, neurobiology and physics. In these fields there are insights to share, and to a certain extent we can work together.
Dalai Lama

Man's main task in life is to give birth to himself. Erich Fromm
Live your life so that the fear of death can never enter your heart. When you arise in the morning, give thanks for the morning light. Give thanks for your life and strength. Give thanks for your food and for the joy of living. And if perchance you see no reason for giving thanks, rest assured the fault is in yourself.
Chief Tecumseh, Shawnee Indian Chief

Your task is not to seek for love, but merely to seek and find all the barriers within yourself that you have built against it. The Buddha
I like your Christ, I do not like your Christians. Your Christians are so unlike your Christ.
Ghandi

If you judge people, you have no time to love them. Mother Teresa
I am no Hindu, but I hold the doctrine of the Hindus concerning a future state (rebirth) to be incomparably more rational, more pious, and more likely to deter men from vice than the horrid opinions inculcated by Christians on punishments without end.
William Jones

Do you have any idea how many lives we must have gone through before we even got the first idea that there is more to life than eating, or fighting, or power in the Flock? A thousand lives, Jon, ten thousand… We choose our next world though what we learn in this one… But you, Jon, learned so much at one time that you didn't have to go through a thousand lives to reach this one.
Richard Bach (Jonathan Livingston Seagull)

The souls must reenter the absolute substance whence they have emerged. But to accomplish this, they must develop all the perfections, the germ of which is planted in them; and if they have not fulfilled this condition during one life, they must commence another, a third, and so forth, until they have acquired the condition which fits them for reunion with God.
Zohar, one of the principal Cabalistic texts

No one should allow his mind to be a vehicle for others to use; he who does not direct his own mind lacks mastery.
Hazrat Inayat Khan

By conquering my mind, I have conquered the whole world.
Sri Guru Granth Sahib

There are plenty of different paths to a deep understanding of the universe.
Blackfoot Proverb

As he thinks in his heart, so he is.
Jewish Proverb

INDEX

About the Author

Philip F. Harris was born in Massachusetts and currently resides in Maine. He received his degree in Political Science from The American University in Washington, D.C. and has worked at every level of government. He is currently employed in special education.

He is co-author of the controversial novel WAKING GOD, coined a "spiritual thriller," which was released 6'06 and will be re-released in '08 with a new publisher. His second novel, A MAINE CHRISTMAS CAROL was released by Cambridge Books in 2'07. His fourth book, RAPING LOUISIANA: A DIARY OF DECEIT was released by Cambridge Books, 9/07. POLARIZING YOUR LIFE TOWARDS PERFECTION is published by Cambridge Books. WAKING GOD BOOK II: THE SACRED ROTA is being released '08 by Literary Road Press.

COLLECTED MESSAGES: GUIDES FOR PERSONAL TRANSFORMATION, BOOKSI, II and III as well as WHAT'S WRONG WITH US ANYWAY? COMMENTARIES ON A

TROUBLED are available from ALL THINGS THAT MATTER PRESS.

Mr. Harris is a nationally syndicated and featured writer for The American Chronicle and has a blog called ALL THINGS THAT MATTER. He is listed as a spiritual growth expert on SelfGrowth.com. He is host of his own Talk Radio show called ALL THINGS THAT MATTER on BlogTalkRadio, http://blogtalkradio.com/pharris. More information on his works can be found at:
http://dickens111.tripod.com/theliteraryworksofphilipharris/

As a certified Holistic Life Coach, Mr. Harris offers guidance to those seeking to take control of their body, mind and spirit at his web site: http://dickens111.tripod.com/newearthhlc

Visit my controversial site, http://humanityontrial.ning.com

OTHER BOOKS BY PHILIP F. HARRIS

A MAINE CHRISTMAS CAROL is more than a retelling of the Dickens classic. It is a contemporary look at modern society with a focus upon young adults. Set in Hallowell, Maine we find old Scrooge replaced by 16 year old TJ. Having lost his father in Iraq, TJ has turned to drugs in an attempt to cope with a world that he feels has spun out of control. TJ alienates himself from his family and friends and his father returns in spirit, like Jacob Marley of old, in an attempt to steer his son from the path of self-destruction. As one reviewer says of the novel, "In the guise of the well loved tale it reminds us of the effects of modern life, its drugs, wars, and poverty, on its people. It gives us the hope and optimism that is much needed in our contemporary world." This novel has received numerous pre-publication reviews that praise its style and content. The English editor of Arabesques Literary and Cultural Review says it is a "biting Christmas fable for out times. Read it, weep, and rejoice." Available from Cambridge Books.

RAPING LOUISIANA: A DIARY OF DECEIT by multi-published author Philip F. Harris is a non-fictional account of one man's observations of the devastation left in the wake of hurricane Katrina. Through the eyes of a driver hired to help in the clean-up, we see a once beautiful and colorful landscape turned into a scene filled with the grays of sewage and chemical-soaked soils, water that is unfit to drink, and the remnants of the lives of thousands scattered along the countryside in heaps of rubble and debris. Observations in the "Diary" tell of the scope of the damage, mishandling of government resources and of the tragedies faced by those who were ill-treated and maligned by the media and public officials. In a tragedy that is still ongoing, the public has been duped into thinking that as a nation, we are ready to deal with the impacts of any natural or man-made emergency. If Louisiana is to offer any lessons, let it be that we are not prepared to face the growing dangers and humanitarian crises that lay ahead in a world under tremendous natural, social, economic, natural, and political pressures. Available from Cambridge Books.

POLARIZING YOUR LIFE TOWARD PERFECTION™ shows how duality consciousness can actually become your servant and a major tool in transforming your life. It provides you with the "fine print" that is often overlooked when trying to use the Law of Attraction to make your dreams a reality. By viewing your life holistically, you can use this book in a practical way to achieve a "total life make-over!" By using the "polarizing" techniques, you will come to the realization that perfection is not something you develop; it is something that you already are. Available from Cambridge Books.

WAKING GOD BOOK I: THE JOURNEY BEGINS-You can dream about life…or you can live it.

"Adam is sleeping, Andrew," Mantrella said. "We are his dream, existing in it and of it. When he comes to realize his own existence, then we will move onto the next spiritual plane. But, and I dread the thought, if he is awakened before the dream has run its course, then we are doomed, all of us."

Waking God explores the role of secret societies in forging the battle lines in the dream and offers insights into the Templars, the Rose Cross, the Teutonic Knights, the Knights of Malta, and the

152

TAROT CODE. The book portrays a world of duality in which one man must take responsibility for his own destiny and not rely on the false promises that all will be well…as long he obeys the dictates of mythical gods.

The line between Michael and Lucifer (a.k.a. Mantrella) was drawn at the beginning of time. The question is, "Who is really on the side of humanity?" Have great myths and conspiracies been perpetuated to keep man in a state of blissful ignorance? In which realm does man's champion really rule? Will there be a Great Awakening or will humanity fade into sleep-induced oblivion?

WAKING GOD BOOK II: THE SACRED ROTA opens doors that many would prefer stay closed. Continuing with the fast paced action of Book I, humanity is beset with growing problems reminiscent of the ancient Biblical plagues. The battle between the Archangel Michael and Mantrella (a.k.a. Lucifer) intensifies as conception of the Old Testament's Adam becomes a certainty. The rise to power of the UN's David Dajjal, a puppet of Michael's, sets the stage for world domination by the Bilderberg Group. New information is revealed about the Tarot Code, the blueprint for man's future spiritual and physical evolution, and the role of the church's Sacred Rota in the epic conspiracy to keep humanity in ignorance and ancient institutions in power. Will the hidden god seed in our DNA be activated with Adam's birth or will secret powers maintain their domination of our destiny?

THE WAKING GOD SERIES IS AVAILABLE THROUGH LITERARY ROAD PRESS.

COLLECTED MESSAGES: GUIDES FOR PERSONAL TRANSFORMATION, BOOKS I, II AND III are available through ALL THINGS THAT MATTER PRESS, http://allthingsthatmatterpress.com, Mobipocket and Amazon.com. Explore alternative medicine, the Law of Attraction, weight reduction, beating cancer, shamanism, the 12th Insight and more from contemporary spiritual leaders.

WHAT'S WRONG WITH US ANYWAY? COMMENTARIES ON A TROUBLED WORLD. Blogs have become the new essays. Read comments on politics, the environment, climate change, education, society and more in the "blog shots" of contemporary society. http://allthingsthatmatterpress.com, Amazon.com and Mobipocket

ALL THINGS THAT MATTER PRESS ™

FOR MORE INFORMATION ON TITLES AVAILABLE FROM
ALL THINGS THAT MATTER PRESS, GO TO
http://allthingsthatmatterpress.com
or contact us at
allthingsthatmatterpress@gmail.com

CPSIA information can be obtained at www.ICGtesting.com
Printed in the USA
269983BV00001B/191/P